Physician's Compensation

Wiley Healthcare Accounting and Finance

John Wiley & Sons has a series of publications to help the healthcare business professional. Take a look at the titles below. Also, visit us at our website: www.wiley.com/accounting, or call Wiley 1-800-272-2100.

Accounting Handbook for Medical Practices
by Rhonda Sides and Michael Roberts
ISBN 0471-37009-6

Guide to Long Term Care Financial Management
by Karen Stevenson Brown
ISBN 0471-35117-2

A Guide to Consulting Services for Emerging Healthcare Organizations
by Robert J. Cimasi
ISBN 0471-31625-3

Healthcare Financial Operations Manual for Independent Practice Associations
by James W. Karling, Reed Tinsley, and Joe D. Havens
ISBN 0471-35927-0 with disk

Performing an Operational and Strategic Assessment for a Medical Practice
by Reed Tinsley and Joe D. Havens
ISBN 0471-29964-2

Valuation of a Medical Practice
by Reed Tinsley, Rhonda W. Sides, and Gregory D. Anderson
ISBN 0471-29965-0

Medical Practice Evaluator: Medical Practice Management & Financial Analysis
Practice management software by Reed Tinsley, Thomas O'Neal, and Thomas McGuiness
ISBN 0471-24548-8

MGMA Physician's Compensation Survey database ISBN 0471-37893-3
MGMA Cost Survey database ISBN 0471-37892-5

Appraisal MD Pro 2000 valuation software ISBN 0471-17138-7

Physician's Compensation

Measurement, Benchmarking, and Implementation

Lucy R. Carter, CPA
Sara S. Lankford, CPA

John Wiley & Sons, Inc
New York • Chichester • Weinheim • Brisbane • Singapore • Toronto

Wiley Healthcare Accounting and Finance

Published simultaneously in Canada.

This publication is designed to provide accurate and authoritative information in
regard to the subject matter covered. It is sold with the understanding that the
publisher is not engaged in rendering legal, accounting, or other professional
services. If legal advice or other expert assistance is required, the services of a
competent professional person should be sought.

Library of Congress Cataloging-in-Publication Data:
Carter, Lucy R.
    Physician's compensation : measurement, benchmarking, and implementation /
Lucy R. Carter, Sara S. Lankford
        p.   ; cm.
    Includes bibliographical reference and index.
    ISBN 0-471-32361-6 (cloth : alk. paper)
    1. Physcians—Salaries, etc.—United States.   2. Compensation management—
United States   I. Lankford, Sara S.   II. Title.
    [DNLM: 1. Group Practice—economics—United States.   2. Group
Practice—legislation & jurisprudence—United States.   3. Group Practice—
organization & administration—United States.   4. Physcian Incentive Plans—
United States.   5. Salaries and Fringe Benefits—United States.   W 92 C324p
2000]
R728.5 .C37 2000

                                                              00-042891

Printed in the United States of America

10 9 8 7 6 5 4 3 2 1

Acknowledgments

This book would not be possible if not for the support and assistance of a lot of great coworkers and families. Thanks to our partners for putting up with "The book"—Charles Young, Sean Roach, Kurt Myers, and Mark Lowhorn. Special thanks to those of you who reviewed several chapters and provided your invaluable insight and experience. Thanks to all the Carter, Young support staff—Stacy Bagshaw, Karen Webster, and Sandy Brooks. Thanks to all the Carter, Young professional staff who participated above and beyond the call of duty—Missy Liverett, Michelle Anderson, John Galloway, John Grigsby, Alicia Reynolds, Felencio Hill, Rob Bass, Terry Utley, Alice Bates, Erica Larvik, Sherry McMahon, Ginger Hartsock, Jason Young, Mike Young, and Chris Jenkins.

Thanks to Peggy Hickman for editorial assistance.

Special thanks to our families for their support of everything we do:

Darrell, Mary and Dale Lankford
Scott and Chris Carter, and Mom—Nancy Reavis

And finally, thanks to all our physician clients who included us in the development of their compensation plans. These projects are always challenging and rewarding.

Lucy R. Carter, CPA   Sara S. Lankford, CPA

About the Authors

Sara S. Lankford CPA, serves as the vice president of the Healthcare Services Division of Carter, Young, Lankford, & Roach, P.C., a certified public accounting firm in Nashville, Tennessee. Ms. Lankford has over 20 years of experience in health care financial management and operations, including her prior employment with Medical Management Sciences (CompMed) as a Regional Financial Analyst.

Ms. Lankford has been active on professional committees for the Tennessee Society of Certified Public Accountants where she chaired the Management Consulting Services Committee and the American Institute of Certified Public Accountants where she served on the Management Consulting Services Technical and Consulting Subcommittee. She also received a certificate of completion from the AICPA as an ISO 9000 Internal Quality Systems Auditor.

Ms. Lankford currently chairs the Legislative Committee for the National CPA Healthcare Advisors Association. She is also a member of the American Health Lawyers Association and the Medical Group Managers Association (national, state, and local chapters).

A frequent speaker, Ms. Lankford has presented numerous programs on medical management and compensation topics. Additionally, Ms. Lankford has authored numerous articles and co-authored the AICPA practice guides, *Guide to Consulting for Dental Practices* and *Guide to Consulting for Long-Term Care Facilities*.

Lucy R. Carter, CPA, is the president of Carter, Young, Lankford, & Roach, P.C. Ms. Carter has 23 years' experience in public accounting, including her previous employment with Cleston Daniels & Associates, P.C. from 1977 to 1985, where she served as the vice president of the Medical Services Division.

Ms. Carter is active on both state and national professional committees. She currently serves as the chair of the Valuation and Litigation Services Committee for the Tennessee Society of Certified Public Accountants and serves on the Group of 100 for the American Institute of Certified Public Accountants. Ms. Carter is also a member of the Nashville Estate Planning Council, the Medical Group Managers Association, and serves on the CEO Roundtable for the Nashville Chamber of Commerce.

Other professional activities include serving on the Board of Directors for Vanderbilt Home Health Care Services, Inc. and on the Board of Directors of McKendree Village. Ms. Carter also serves as treasurer for Community Child Care Services, a non-profit child care center for low income families.

A frequent speaker, Ms. Carter has presented numerous programs on medical management and compensation topics. Additionally, Ms. Carter has authored numerous articles and currently serves as an editorial advisor for the *Practicing CPA*.

Contents

Introduction   1

Chapter One   **Factors Impacting Physician Compensation**   **5**
               Managed Care   6
               Product Development   7
               Financial Implications   7
               Consumer Demands   10
               Merger and Integration of Practices   14
               Government Regulation   17

Chapter Two   **The Shrinking Pie**   **20**
               Reimbursement Trends   21
               Medicare   21
               Participation versus Nonparticipation   22
               Medicaid   24
               Managed Care/Commercial Payors   25
               Overhead Trends   26
               Competition and the Impact on Physician
               Compensation   26
               Disease of Me, Defeat of Us   27

Chapter Three **Defining the Pie**   **28**
               Net Cash Available   28
               Net Income   29
               "Eat What You Kill"   30
               Bonus versus Incentive   31
               Financial Reporting   31

Chapter Four	**Regulatory Considerations in Physician Compensation Arrangements**	**32**
	Tax-Exempt Organizations	33
	Recruitment Agreements	33
	Tax-Exempt Financing	35
	Fraud and Abuse	37
	Antikickback Statute	37
	Stark I and Stark II	44
	Fair Market Value Compensation	52
	De Minimis Compensation	53
	Discounts	54
Chapter Five	**Four Basic Principles of Compensation**	**56**
Principle #1:	Physicians in the Group Must Trust the Formula	56
Principle #2:	The Formula Must Be Clearly Understood	57
Principle #3:	The Formula Must Be Equitable	59
Principle #4:	Group Incentives Must Be Promoted	59
Chapter Six	**Tax Considerations for Physician Compensation**	**62**
	General Partnerships	62
	Limited Liability Companies	63
	Professional Corporations	64
Chapter Seven	**Employment Agreements**	**75**
Chapter Eight	**Base Salary**	**83**
	Preparing the Budget	85
	Revenues	86
	Expenses	88
	Capital Budgets	89
	Determining Base	90
Chapter Nine	**Incentive Compensation**	**94**
Chapter Ten	**Physician Benefit Plans**	**101**
Chapter Eleven	**Measuring Productivity**	**109**
	Gross Charges	109
	Adjusted Charges	110
	Collections	111
	Relative Value Units	112

	Weighted Average Production	112
	Points System	112
	Other Methods	113
Chapter Twelve	**Relative Value Units**	**114**
	Work RVUs	116
	Practice Expense RVUs	118
	Malpractice RVUs	119
	Geographic Practice Cost Index (GPCI)	119
	Conversion Factors	120
Chapter Thirteen	**Using Relative Value Units to Measure Productivity**	**121**
	RVUs in Capitation	123
	Costs per RVU	124
Chapter Fourteen	**Cost Allocation**	**125**
	Direct Expenses	126
	Equal Expenses	127
	Utilization	128
	Volume	128
	Prior Year Allocation Method	129
	Stark Revenues	131
Chapter Fifteen	**Administering the Compensation Plan**	**133**
Chapter Sixteen	**Academic Group Practice Compensation Models**	**139**
Chapter Seventeen	**Physician Integration Systems**	**145**
	Management Services Organization Model	146
	Foundation Model	148
	Hospital-Owned Physcian Practice Model (Integrated Delivery System)	150
Chapter Eighteen	**Compensating the Physician CEO**	**155**
	Medical Administration	160
	Evaluation and Management of Physicians	160
	Committee Responsibilities	161
	Quality Management	161
	Miscellaneous Duties	161

Chapter Nineteen   Physician Compensation Case Studies   164
                      Case 1: ABC Internal Medicine Practices   165
                      Case 2: XYZ Surgical Group   170

Chapter Twenty   Common Pitfalls   176

Appendix A Sample Physician Encounter Budget and Comparison   179

Appendix B Sample Practice Budget   180

Appendix C Sample Financial Statements   183

Appendix D Revenue Ruling 97–13   188

Appendix E Glossary of Terms   197

References   201

Index   205

Introduction

The constantly changing and dramatically shifting framework of the health-care delivery system in the United States has required physician groups to revisit and revise traditional compensation methodologies. The "good old days" of fee-for-service revenue are gone. In the currently pervasive managed care environment, revenue generally comes in the form of discounted fee for service (FFS) and/or capitation rates. Physician compensation and incentive packages must be restructured and find new focus as a result.

Just as market forces were a major factor in driving healthcare reform across the country during the 1990s, market forces also were behind the fundamental changes in how physicians receive compensation. The primary market forces pushing changes in the healthcare delivery system during the past ten years have been escalating healthcare expenditures, projections for future spending due to an aging population, and the increasing numbers of uninsured Americans. These forces are still at work and will be for some time to come. In fact, the inescapable pressures created by an aging population will increase greatly during the next 20, 30 and even 40 years. And while government is keenly aware of all these market forces, it is the private sector that has taken the lead in making changes to the healthcare delivery system.

In October 1993 President Bill Clinton introduced to Congress the most sweeping healthcare reform package (the President's Health Security Act) since the Roosevelt era. Built on the concept of "managed competition," the Clinton package was designed to organize physicians, hospitals, and insurers into competing accountable health plans (AHPs) that would contract with health alliances (purchasing cooperatives) to offer standardized packages of health benefits for fixed annual capitation rates.

President Clinton's healthcare reform package did not gain support from either party in Congress. However, the private sector did respond by devising its own strategies and programs to decrease healthcare spending, increase quality, and provide access to care for all American citizens. The result was an increase in managed care products and organizations via mergers and integrations of healthcare providers and payors. And while Congress may not have supported the president's Healthcare Reform bill, legislation was introduced and subsequently passed that would affect the income levels, compensation packages, and organizational infrastructure for all medical service providers.

Regulatory requirements are the "big stick" that government is wielding over physician compensation plans. Although Stark regulations (named for their author, Congressman Pete Stark) are the best-publicized laws that specifically address compensation in group practices, other provisions of the Medicare statute, such as the reassignment rules, must be considered in the design of any compensation plan. While certain physician compensation models may minimize the risk from noncompliance with federal and state regulations, their design actually may discourage the behavior that is essential to the financial success of the practice and its long-term stability. Some practice managers ruefully express their dilemma as "Comply and perish."

However, since the market forces are not going away for a long, long time to come, it is imperative to design physician compensation models that will meet the immediate and long-term needs of the practice and comply with multiplying regulations. Without addressing the compensation needs of physicians, the practice will fail and ultimately the overall healthcare delivery system will be weakened.

Physician compensation is more than money. Physician compensation is a powerful strategic tool that can be used to direct behavior. An effective compensation model will empower the group to achieve levels of performance that it might not achieve otherwise. Conversely, a compensation model may include incentives that create the I'd-rather-play-golf syndrome whereby individuals are guaranteed compensation without a required work effort.

In the old fee-for-service environment, increases in production or in fees charged for services would result in a direct increase in revenues, hence production-based compensation was accepted as the norm. The primary concern of a total production compensation plan was in the allocation of expenses. However, the goals for physician compensation plans have shifted from encouraging pure productivity to include such initiatives as resource conservation, patient satisfaction, and quality of care (outcomes measurement). Physician compensation plans of the present and the future must be structured to tackle effectively the specific requirements of the group while considering the market and regulatory environment of the industry.

The challenge is to establish a plan that will promote alignment with group incentives while encouraging physician motivation and complying with government regulations. The mission of the practice must be well established. The compensation incentives should be structured properly to support the mission, or both will fail.

In order to achieve physician buy-in to any change in an existing compensation system, there must be a clear understanding of the incentives. The physician members of the group must understand clearly what they are being paid to do as well as the specific behaviors the compensation model is trying to measure. Individuals must have a strong sense that the methodology used to determine their compensation is a valid definition of the value of their work product. Although "fairness" is a qualitative word, there must be a consensus in the group that the plan is "fair."

Consider this quote from a National Health Lawyers Association seminar presenter from 1994: "Partnership is a term describing a group of individuals who blame each other for the unfair amount of their own income."

Behind the wit of this quote lies an important truth. Physicians must be actively involved in the development and administration of the compensation plan. Physicians must trust the plan and the data used in computations. Informative and timely financial and budget data are also necessary. Systems must be in place to allow for administration of the plan. While the management theory of "KISS" (keep it simple, stupid) is a great concept, unfortunately it does not usually work in the design of compensation plans.

Although all compensation plans contain some universal components, no one compensation model will work for every practice. The specific dynamics of each group and its members must be considered in designing an effective plan.

Never forget that the appropriate physician compensation is essential to the financial success of the group practice. Never forget that without a compensation plan that is supported and understood by the physicians in the group, eventually the practice will fail.

Always remember that compensation plans serve as the foundation for individual physicians to succeed in their profession.

A well-designed, flexible plan that also complies with government regulations will guide the practice to a financially healthy future. Flexibility in the compensation system may not provide a high level of satisfaction to individuals because of the group trust factor, but it does allow the group to meet financial needs in a predefined manner. Group members should understand and agree that the plan will be modified on an ongoing basis to meet these needs.

Anyone faced with the task of developing compensation plans for physicians faces a difficult task. Whether you approach the task as a physician, consultant, practice administrator, accountant, or lawyer, you are faced with the dilemma of meeting seemingly conflicting needs. The compensation plan must comply with government regulations as it meets the financial requirements of the practice. The plan must support the greater goals of the group as it meets the needs of individuals. Additionally, the compensation plan should inspire positive immediate behavior while incorporating the flexibility to respond to the shifting healthcare environment.

This book addresses the issues surrounding this dilemma. It seeks to provide a base of understanding of all the factors affecting development of physician compensation plans, but it also seeks to guide the reader through the process by identifying resources, tools, and models. Humility based on experience dictates that no one compensation plan will meet every need or be equivalent to other plans, yet certain universal components and regulations will apply to all.

This book is intended primarily to serve as a handbook of resources and of compensation plan components for the closely held physician group practice. However, it also includes discussions regarding academic settings and other integrated delivery systems.

This book brings no promises except one. The design of an effective, equitable, and flexible physician compensation package will be a challenge but will bring financial rewards and stability to the practice and its members.

CHAPTER ONE

Factors Impacting
Physician Compensation

"People get what they deserve."
—Folk Wisdom

The simple bit of folk wisdom just quoted may not apply to physician compensation in the current managed care environment. While physicians *should* get the financial compensation that they deserve, it is increasingly difficult to determine and provide "deserved" compensation because of the dramatic changes in reimbursement patterns.

These changes are a result of increases in the number of managed care payor contracts, consumer demands, merging and integration of group practices, and increases in government regulations aimed at reducing healthcare spending. All of these factors must be considered in developing physician compensation plans. As a result, compensation plans have become more complex as groups attempt to respond to and comply with market realities while striving to ensure that physicians get what they deserve.

Before a compensation plan can be developed, it is important to understand the concepts underlying the healthcare delivery system today, to know how it got here and to be aware of where it is going. Revenues drive salaries in any industry, so it is crucial to understand the various mechanisms by which physicians receive those revenues.

How should one begin to develop a physician compensation plan? We recommend a short review of the factors at work in the healthcare delivery system that impact physician compensation.

MANAGED CARE

Managed care—or "mangled care," as many providers describe the system—is a healthcare delivery system that delivers healthcare services through contractual arrangements between providers and third-party payors. Prior to the mid-1990s, physicians provided healthcare services to patients under verbal contracts between physician and patient. The physician-patient relationship was built on trust. Services provided were rarely questioned as to the "medical necessity" and were paid at face value (fee for service).

As of year 2000, such arrangements are generally a thing of the past. Today physicians primarily provide services to patients under a contractual arrangement with a third-party payor or organization. The system attempts to control costs by employing reduced reimbursement and by controls over the quality and frequency of services provided. Among the payment methods included in these contracts are:

- Deeply discounted fee-for-service payments: This payment method reimburses providers for each service after the service has been provided (delivered) *minus* an agreed-upon percentage off the provider's usual, customary, and reasonable fee or at a percentage of the Medicare fee schedule.

- Negotiated fee schedule payments: The managed care organization establishes a fee schedule, which may be based on discounting its usual and customary charges, or established fee schedules based on a relative value scale.

- Capitation, withholds, and risk/reward sharing: Capitation payments are made to providers in advance of the service at a predetermined per member, per month amount regardless of the level of service provided. These payments may, in turn, be reduced by a withhold, which is a reserve at the payor level to offset losses or pay out surpluses.

- Control-of-utilization methods: These reimbursement strategies seek to control costs in two primary ways.

  1. Referral and authorization requirements: Services must be approved by the managed care organization prior to the service being delivered or payment will be denied.

  2. Closed panels: The number of providers are limited by the managed care plans.

PRODUCT DEVELOPMENT

Previously, almost every patient was covered by some form of health insurance plan that paid the physician a fee for service set by the plan. No more. Today the managed care system is comprised of different types of healthcare payment *products* and organizations, with new entities and products being developed daily to meet changing market forces. Physicians have little if any influence over the types of products that are sold in the marketplace. They are restricted by government regulations in their ability to develop organizations that address managing care in response to marketplace forces. The result is seen in the financial impact on the practice. Revenues have been reduced and expenses increased due to multiplying administrative responsibilities.

Payors determine product development in response to consumer demands. The following products and organizations that administer those products include:

- Indemnity plans: Traditional non–managed care products. Physicians are paid at the fee charged for a service provided by the insurance plan.
- Discounted fee-for-service plans: These operate through preferred provider organizations (PPO) or directly with physician(s).
- Capitated plans: These plans work directly with the provider or through an organization, such as a health maintenance organization (HMO) or independent practice association (IPA).
- Point-of-service plans (POS): These plans have contracts allowing for discounted fees for service at different rates for obtaining service outside the assigned network of physicians in a product.

FINANCIAL IMPLICATIONS

Physicians may receive payment from these products as individuals or as members of managed care organizations. Whether receiving payment as individuals or as managed care organization members, physicians will be impacted by the concept of "sharing financial risk," which is included in most products. Sharing of financial risk is a complicated concept. Furthermore, it is uncertain how the physician can assist a payor in decreasing costs and creating profit pools to influence the impact of financial risk.

Depending on the product, the contract may provide for not only a discounted fee for service but also for withholds of a specified percentage. Under this scenario, the physician accepts a discount off the usual and customary charge and agrees to a percentage of reimbursement to be withheld from payments by the payor. These "withholds" represent a reserve to cover deficits or surpluses of the plan. Any "profits" or "surpluses" of the plan for each year are to be distributed to the physicians participating with that plan based on whatever method the plan develops. This policy obviously creates a financial unknown for the physician or group practice. In general, groups do not include in revenue projections any returns from this withhold. Discounted fee for service otherwise provides a traceable and somewhat predictable method of projecting revenues. However, as the number of plans in which a physician participates increases, the complexity of monitoring the revenues from those plans also increases. (Note: Revenue projections are discussed at length in Chapter 8 along with issues associated with physician incentives.)

Discounted fee for service has been a major factor in reducing reimbursement to physicians. The result has been that physicians are providing the same services for reduced rates while incurring higher costs for doing business. If the group practice participates in only indemnity and discounted fee-for-service products, determining the level of production the physicians need to maintain in order to realize a level of reimbursement that will cover overhead and result in a compensation package that is satisfactory to the physicians in the group is the primary issue in the development of the plan.

Increases in capitated prepaid revenue products have had a significant impact on physicians' compensation and add a new dimension to the development of the plan, as the incentives are different. Capitated payors typically compensate the practice, the practice network, or the integrated delivery system on an assigned per member per month (PMPM) basis irrespective of the actual number of patient visits. The PMPM is determined actuarially by the managed care payor or HMO. Capitated plans are based on a sharing-of-risk theory whereby utilization can make or break the providers of service.

Capitated plans do provide a benefit to the practice by providing a steady stream of income. If managed properly through efficient utilization, capitated arrangements can be profitable for both the practice and the physician employee. The key to profitability depends on the ability of the practice to secure an adequate PMPM reimbursement rate and its ability to control costs and manage utilization.

In a capitated plan, primary care practices typically are compensated a fixed monthly dollar amount based on the number of patients (covered lives, members, or enrollees) assigned to the group practice or individuals in the group. Specialists may be paid a capitated PMPM amount based on the total number of patients in the plan or may be reimbursed on a discounted fee-for-service basis.

Managing utilization and resources in the practice provides the greatest challenge as groups move from a fee-for-service environment to capitation. In a fee-for-service environment, increased patient visits equate to increased revenue. The opposite is true in a capitated arrangement. Overutilization of services decreases the capitated profit margin. The physician group must provide the clinical management and protocols to ensure quality care while managing utilization.

In a capitated environment, the compensation system cannot be based on incentives that motivate the physicians to increase patient visits. Nor should incentives be included that encourage physicians to refer patients to specialists rather than continuing personally to provide continuing care. The key is to keep physicians productive by providing services at an efficient cost level. The system must be retooled to stress resource and utilization management. The underlying compensation plan philosophy must be one that encourages conservation of services while maintaining quality patient care.

In addition, prepaid revenues complicate the level of reporting necessary to provide the data for allocating revenues and expenses to the providers of service. Data will be needed on a per-plan basis; cost and utilization data within the group also are needed. Services provided should be tracked based on the group's fee-for-service equivalent charge. Doing so generally serves as the basis for determining the cost of providing patient care by individual physicians.

Although capitation plans have increased over the past several years as payors attempt to manage rising healthcare costs, in most practices the percentage of capitated revenues is still minimal. The *Cost Survey: 1999 Report Based on 1998 Data* by the Medical Group Management Association (MGMA) indicates that approximately 82 percent of the practices included in the survey have less than 10 percent in capitated revenues. Sixty-two percent have no capitation. The geographic area with the heaviest penetration of capitation is the western section, where 28 percent of the reporting practices had 11 to 50 percent capitation.

In a pure fee-for-service environment, many physician groups adopt an eat-what-you-kill mentality. Compensation models are designed to encourage physicians to maximize the number of encounters or procedures performed. Simply stated, the more the physician works, the more money he or she can expect to make. In a low capitation environment—where capitation represents less than 15 percent of revenue—the small percentage of capitation rarely justifies a payment system that does anything more than encourage productivity with incentives.

As the percentage of capitated revenues to total revenue increases in the medical practice, the focus of the compensation system shifts proportionately from production to other factors, such as utilization management, patient satisfaction, and group performance. Compensation plans in this environment include a salary for the physician based on predetermined criteria and a performance-based incentive. Utilization management becomes a key factor and a strong contributor to group profitability in practices with capitated revenues in excess of 50 percent. Establishing quality protocols and monitoring clinical outcomes are key factors in managing care.

Financial incentives must be structured and aligned properly to drive and sustain the behaviors needed to prosper in a managed care environment. Capitation has a direct impact on the income available for physician compensation according to the MGMA's 1999 Report. As the percent of capitated revenue increases in specialty practices, the median compensation per physician drops substantially. For specialty practices with no capitation, the median income is $296,595. As capitated revenues approach 10 percent of total revenue, median compensation for specialists drops to $282,913. At 50 percent capitation, the median declines to $212,750; at full capitation, specialists' median compensation drops to $196,771.

The effect of capitation on primary care income is less pronounced. Median primary care compensation in practices with no capitated revenue is $143,930. At 10 percent or less capitation, compensation declines slightly, to $142,303. As capitation approaches 50 percent, median primary care compensation declines to $135,000. Interestingly at full capitation, compensation increases to $141,242.

Reimbursement techniques utilized by managed care products and organizations create the need for determining performance measures based on the provisions of each plan. Developing appropriate incentives to create the behavior necessary to result in profitable contract performance is an integral component of any compensation plan.

CONSUMER DEMANDS

Health-care reform initiatives have placed a great emphasis on quality of care and on fraud and abuse in the healthcare industry. While limited healthcare initiatives have been enacted by the federal government, discussion about them has prompted a shift in the patient/provider relationship. Patients have become consumers of healthcare services. Armed with ammunition from the government, private insurance industry, and nonprofit organizations developed to further the quality of healthcare, consumers are prepared to question the qualifications of anyone participating in the provision of healthcare services to themselves, family, and friends.

President Clinton's Health Security Act of 1993 stated that "the American health care system, as a whole, is in deep crisis." It went on to say that "today's American health care system falls short of providing high quality care and choices for all Americans." The act identified numerous problems with the healthcare system. While most Americans had a general sense that all was not well with the healthcare system, the enumeration of its woes had a strong impact on consumer awareness and concerns. The following is a summary of some of the problems described in the act.

- Lack of security: The act stated that 37 million Americans have no insurance and another 22 million have inadequate coverage. Becoming ill or living with a chronic medical condition can mean losing insurance coverage or not being able to obtain it.

- Rising costs: Rising health costs mean lower wages, higher prices for goods and services, and higher taxes. As a result of rising costs, more and more Americans have given up insurance altogether because the premiums have become prohibitively expensive. In addition, many small companies either cannot afford insurance at all in the current system or have had to cut benefits or profits in order to provide insurance to their employees.

- Quality threatened: The act stated that no one is accountable for the performance of the healthcare system—not hospitals, physicians, other providers, or health insurers. While quality care should mean promoting good health, our system waits until people are sick before it starts to work. Furthermore, healthcare is biased toward specialty care and gives inadequate attention to cost-effective primary and preventive care. In addition, consumers cannot compare doctors and hospitals because reliable quality information is not available to them.

  Moreover, the act asserted that healthcare providers often do not have enough information on which treatments work best and are most cost effective. Healthcare treatment patterns vary widely without detectable effects on health status. The act stated that our medical malpractice system does little to promote quality. Fear of litigation forces providers to practice defensive medicine—ordering inappropriate tests and procedures to protect against lawsuits. Often truly negligent providers are not disciplined, and many victims of real malpractice are not compensated for their injuries.

As mentioned in the introduction, this act was not enacted. However, it stirred national debate. In addition, all of the issues addressed in the act have been considered in the development of products available on the market today and in legislation based on consumer awareness.

Both the government and private sector insurance companies are encouraging patients—the consumers—to ask more questions about their providers of care. In response to this movement, some physicians include in their compensation plans a component based on patient satisfaction or outcomes. Although patient satisfaction may be somewhat quantifiable based on surveys, outcomes measurement is a complex concept that is not easily determined.

All of these discussions have led to a search for the definition of quality. Bruce C. Vladeck, past administrator of the Health Care Financing Administration (HCFA), provided HCFA's definition of quality during his 1997 remarks at the National Roundtable on Health Care Quality sponsored by the National Institute of Medicine. He said: "Quality of care is the extent to which health care and health-related services result in desired outcomes and greater satisfaction with care for the populations and individuals we serve. . . . Our definition incorporates several other themes that reflect HCFA's mission . . . and it explicitly includes beneficiary satisfaction as part of the quality calculation."

In support of this mission, under Vladeck's administration, HCFA played a major role in developing and adopting the HEDIS 3.0 system. HEDIS stands for Health Plan Employer Data and Information Set. It is a set of standardized performance measures designed to ensure that purchasers and consumers have the information they need to reliably compare the performance of managed health care plans. The performance measures in HEDIS are related to many significant public health issues, such as cancer, heart disease, smoking, asthma, and diabetes. HEDIS provides purchasers and consumers with an unprecedented ability both to evaluate the quality of different health plans along a variety of important dimensions and to make their plan decisions based on demonstrated value rather than simply on cost.

HEDIS is sponsored by the National Committee for Quality Assurance (NCQA). The NCQA is a private, not-for-profit organization dedicated to improving the quality of healthcare. The organization's primary activities are assessing and reporting on the quality of the nation's managed care plans. NCQA's efforts have led to partnerships and collaborative efforts with many states, the federal government, employer and consumer groups, and many of the nation's leading corporations and business coalitions. As of December 31, 1999, the states of New York, Ohio, Alabama, Tennessee, and Iowa all have established deadlines for health plans serving state employees to obtain NCQA accreditation. At the federal level, NCQA is working with the U.S. Office of Personnel Management on methods to provide federal employees with additional information on health plan quality to assist in the selection of health plans.

NCQA's mission is to provide information that enables purchasers and consumers of managed healthcare to distinguish among plans based on quality, thereby allowing them to make more informed healthcare purchasing decisions. Using information from NCQA's accreditation program in combination with HEDIS data, the most complete view of health plan quality is available to guide choice among competing health plans. Additional research and background information may be found at the NCQA web site: www.ncqa.org.

A federal effort is under way to measure and report physician outcomes. On May 7, 1998, the Department of Health and Human Services (DHHS) published in the *Federal Register* the Notice of Proposed Rulemaking (NPRM) for the National Provider Identifier (NPI). The NPRM recommended the adoption of the NPI as the standard healthcare provider identifier. The final rule is expected to be released in June 2000 with a compliance date of December 2002. Even though all physicians currently must have a provider number and unique provider identification number (UPIN) and must submit claims for payment using these numbers, a system is not in place to utilize these numbers to measure outcomes or performance in the numerous plans in which an individual physician may participate. Therefore, the National Provider Identification Number (NPIN) is being developed to use as a standard healthcare provider number to be used for filing claims under all health plans. This information combined with the NCQA and HEDIS data will provide a device for performance and outcomes measurement for physician services and healthcare plans.

On the private side, health plans are adopting "quality indexes." Pacificare Health System on a semiannual basis sends 1.5 million enrollees a report outlining how their clinic ranks compared with other clinics in the system. The "quality index" ranks medical groups in 28 indicators of care in three categories: clinical quality, service quality, and administrative services. The better-performing providers are rewarded with a higher capitation rate. Insurance companies have begun to use physician profiling not only in deciding who participates in a panel but also in contract negotiations and setting payment rates. Profiling involves comparing physician performance on utilization of services, adherence to clinical guidelines, and other measures. The goal is to identify providers who are "outliers"—who use more services or have higher costs than other physicians—and urge them to make changes that lower costs. Physicians will need the information systems in place that provide these data to profile their own practices and include these "quality" indicators in their future compensation plans.

If there was any doubt about the linkage of quality of care to reimbursement, consider the remarks made by Nancy-Ann DeParle, administrator for the HCFA, on December 17, 1998. Speaking at an all-staff meeting on the HCFA Strategic Plan, she made the following statements:

"As our mission statement articulates what we do, our vision statement articulates how we want to be seen—leading the nation's health care system toward improved health for all. This vision reflects our increasing appreciation of our role as the largest health insurer in the U.S. . . . As the largest health insurer in the nation and as a public purchaser of care, HCFA plays a leadership role in developing and reining payment systems, data standards, quality indicators and innovative ways of informing beneficiaries about health care choices. Like it or not, what we do influences the whole U.S. health care system. We must be intentional on how we use that influence."

It is apparent from the remarks of both Vladeck as HCFA administrator in 1997 and DeParle as HCFA administrator in 1998 that the mission of the federal government is to include quality in some manner as a component of reimbursement. Defining the quality assurance components of a compensation plan will be specific to any one practice or specialty. Defining the measure of the quality assurance will be a dilemma. Defining the weight that these measures have on total compensation will be a greater dilemma.

Today a very small percentage of physician practices include patient satisfaction and quality as components of compensation plans. In the coming few years, the compensation plans of virtually every practice will have to include these components based on the actions of HCFA and state governments in coordinating performance measures with the HEDIS and NCQA surveys.

MERGER AND INTEGRATION OF PRACTICES

> *Everything should be made as simple as possible, but not simpler.*
> —Albert Einstein

The merger and integration of practices has impacted physician compensation models significantly. In 1965 there were 4,000 group practices, while today the number exceeds 19,000. The numbers and size of these groups makes compensation plan analysis, design, and revision essential. Underlying this process is the need to keep compensation plans as simple, understandable, and equitable as possible while addressing all the emerging regulations and shifting requirements of the practice and its members. The compensation plan designer walks a fine line. Einstein's advice to keep it as simple as possible should be heeded, tempered by the wisdom of King Solomon: Don't share your baby in such a way that you no longer have a baby—that is, don't try to meet the needs of each physician member at the expense of the overall practice.

Solo physicians who merge with others are faced with the issue of how to share income and expenses that previously was totally theirs. Typically, compensation plans developed as a result of mergers between one or more solo practitioners will result in the eat-what-you-kill mentality in an attempt to mirror premerger operational results.

Issues may soon surface concerning the allocation of expenses, however. The division of overhead becomes especially sensitive in mergers of solo practices where the physicians have significantly different levels of patient visits, case mix, payor mix, and/or provide different subspecialties of medicine. As the practice matures, payor mix considerations may arise in the scheduling and allocation of patient visits. As mentioned previously, pure productivity formulas are not effective in a heavily capitated practice.

As with the merger and integration of solo practitioners, group practice mergers also raise a host of compensation issues. When groups merge, the new entity must face the task of bringing together diverse plans into a new combined plan that will achieve the objectives of the combined group. Most likely each of the merging entities will utilize a different methodology for sharing income and expenses. At a time when the merging practices are dealing with significant operational changes, revisions to the compensation models can be particularly stressful and increase an already existing level of anxiety and tension.

The first step in compensation plan design for merging groups is for the group to establish a strategic plan and mission. The group must decide its direction and goals in order for incentives to be established in the compensation plan to achieve those goals. The plan should be analyzed to determine if it complies with the mission statement and fosters the group mentality regarding practice operations, quality of care, and hours worked. As the merging practice matures, incentives can be adjusted as strategies and requirements of the organization change.

The key to long-term group success will depend on the ability of the practice to align individual behaviors with the goals of the practice. To achieve this goal, the compensation system must reward appropriate behaviors with incentives. Issues related to compensation that must be addressed include but are not limited to:

- Production
- Capitation
- Call coverage
- Administrative compensation
- Seniority
- Other physician compensation such as pension contributions

To proceed with a merger, many times groups postpone dealing with compensation issues. A delay in dealing with compensation, however, can be the death knell for merging groups. The wise practice will address compensation head on and reach a consensus on a combined compensation plan before the merger. If the combining group cannot reach consensus, the best alternative is to postpone the merger. Disagreements over compensation can lead to group breakups, which can be financially devastating for all involved.

In an attempt to deal effectively with managed care, more and more multispecialty practices are merging. Specialists have sought alliances with primary care physicians in an attempt to preserve their referral sources and "gatekeeper" relationships.

However, mergers between multispecialty groups can present additional problems. Multispecialty merger conflicts can arise purely over cultural issues. Historically specialists have occupied elite roles in the medical field, in some cases, commanding compensation far in excess of their primary care counterparts.

To illustrate the compensation disparity, consider that the median compensation for primary care physicians is $139,244, as reported in the MGMA 1999 Report. The median compensation reported for specialists was $231,993.

The emergence of managed care has, to some extent, caused a role reversal as the position of "gatekeeper" for primary care physicians has become established. Specialists are now dependent on primary care physicians for referral reimbursement. According to the Medical Group Managers Association survey, specialists are willing to pay for this alliance. Specialists in single-specialty groups reflected median compensation of $299,648 while their counterparts in multispecialty groups earned a median of $201,312. Conversely, primary care physicians reported median compensation of $137,716 in single specialty practices, whereas the median income increased to $139,591 for multispecialty practices.

Combining cultural differences in multispecialty practice mergers is nothing short of forming a United Nations group. Add to these differences the combination of compensation systems and you may create World War III. Developing a system of revenue and expense sharing in these groups presents multiple problems. Combining compensation plans in a multispecialty practice is an extremely delicate undertaking, due to the differing group styles and operational practices. For example, assume a family practice group joins forces with a surgical specialty. Allocating overhead may become a key factor due to the differences in utilization of office facilities and supplies.

Should an anesthesiologist in a multispecialty group pick up expenses based on a percent of collections? Obviously this specialist would not utilize resources within the clinic setting for patient visits. The specialty does, however, generate a higher level of collections than a primary care physician. By using collections as a measure of resource utilization, the anesthesiologist would be allocated an unreasonable amount of expenses.

GOVERNMENT REGULATION

The numerous laws that affect income distribution further complicate developing compensation systems for physician organizations. The list of those laws includes:

- Antikickback law
- Stark I and II
- Tax-exemption rules contained in the Internal Revenue Code
- Tax-exempt bond financing rules
- Corporate practice of medicine
- Antitrust laws

In a group practice owned 100 percent by the physicians providing services, the Stark laws (Ethics in Patient Referrals Act of 1989) provide the greatest challenge to the development of compensation formulas. Stark prevents physicians from receiving compensation based on the value or volume of designated health services (ancillary income). Stark can have a traumatic effect on existing groups as well as merging practices as they revise and design compensation plans to comply with the law's regulations. Chapter 4 is dedicated to the issues involved with Stark laws in determining compensation systems. Each of the above-listed laws is also discussed in later chapters regarding both their implications to group practice and, to a limited basis, the concerns of physician organizations with nonphysician capital partners.

The tempo of change in healthcare is likely to become faster-paced in the years ahead. Managed care, mergers, integration, and regulations are expected to take on new faces in the new millennium as the cost of healthcare services continues to rise. Medicare reimbursement regulations will continue to change on a daily basis. Payors will continue to merge and restructure products to meet the demands of society.

Cost will be one of the factors setting this stepped-up tempo of change. For the first time since the early 1990s, large employers are now encountering a double-digit increase in their healthcare costs, according to the annual *Towers Perrin Healthcare Cost Survey*. The most recent survey, which was released January 10, 2000, projects that health benefit plans' costs will increase by approximately 12 percent in 2000. The survey finds that employees will contribute an average of $40 a month (21 percent of the total cost of their coverage) in 2000 for employee-only coverage. At least 90 percent of respondents expect double-digit increases in healthcare costs for the next several years. These figures are based on responses from survey participants, who were asked to provide their 1999 and 2000 per capita premium costs for insured health and dental plans and premium costs for insured health and dental plans and premium equivalents (i.e., estimated benefit and administrative costs) for self-insured plans.

The Towers Perrin survey reports that the large upturn in healthcare costs is a complex problem with several causes. The rising costs of prescription drugs due to increased demand, higher utilization of healthcare services by a gradually aging population, and Medicare cutbacks that shifted costs from the government employers are believed to be key factors in the rise. As the insurance industry and government debate the issues and reform their policies and practices to provide beneficiaries with care at the lowest cost, it is clear that providers, physicians, and suppliers of healthcare services need to revise their strategies as a means of survival.

Physicians and their management teams must constantly be aware of all these activities. Even Einstein's insight has limitations and is subject to revisions. The "simple as possible, but not simpler" compensation plan of today may be inappropriate tomorrow.

The information provided in this book is intended to serve as a basis for generating discussion and ideas for developing a compensation system that meets the objectives and goals of a group given a set of circumstances at any given time. Changes in the market and group infrastructure will require further analysis and research.

CHAPTER TWO

The Shrinking Pie

When the pie shrinks, the table manners change!
—Brian D. Wong, MD, MPH

Declining physician compensation in a medical group can cause volatile reactions. When physician compensation declines, a financial biopsy of the practice may be necessary to determine the cause.

An objective analysis should focus on the following:

- Analysis of physician productivity

  Has physician productivity declined?

  How does individual productivity compare with established medians (i.e., MGMA)?

  How is production defined (charges, collections, relative value units (RVUs), number of patients)?

  How does practice productivity compare with established medians (i.e., those provided by the Medical Group Management Association [MGMA])?

- Analysis of group spending

  Is practice overhead increasing disproportionately to increases in productivity?

  For instance, is productivity declining while expenses are increasing?

  Are services provided requiring large outlays of cash, such as chemotherapy drugs?

- Analysis of physician compensation

  Are physicians paid more than their contribution to the practice?

Does the group borrow money to fund compensation?

What is the underlying theory of the existing compensation plan?

Do all physicians participate in call pay?

Do all physicians receive the same benefits?

Do all physicians work the same schedules?

How are expenses allocated?

As the compensation pie continues to shrink, medical practices will be forced to examine critically all facets of practice operations. Physician-owners must begin to accept the harsh realities of ownership—owners get paid last. Basically, there are no guarantees of income in a group practice. The groups that succeed will objectively address operational issues both clinical and administrative. Groups that choose to ignore the warning signs and symptoms of an ailing practice may be headed for terminal disease with no cure.

REIMBURSEMENT TRENDS

Prior to managed care, physician compensation models were based on the philosophy that more production equaled more revenue and more revenue equated to increased physician compensation. If physicians wanted to increase their compensation, they simply increased the number of patients seen or increased fees. Operational efficiencies were not a concern as fee increases could be used to cover additional costs. Additionally, competition was not a concern. It has been said that physicians could make money carrying cash in a wheelbarrow during a windstorm. This mentality was a direct result of the methods of reimbursement for healthcare services.

Times have changed. Managed care (discounted fee for service and capitation) is a reality. Currently, there are over 1,600 managed care organizations that account for an approximate 46 percent of group practice revenues. In most cases, managed care organizations negotiate with providers for deep discounts in fee-for-service revenues for the privilege of inclusion in their provider panel. (Some plans reimburse below the Medicare rates.)

MEDICARE

Medicare is the nation's largest payor of healthcare services. On average, Medicare revenues comprise approximately 22 percent of medical group revenues. In the 1990s, physicians experienced a dramatic change in the way they were reimbursed for fee-for-service patients. Authorized by law in 1989, the national physician fee schedule payment system marked the most important change for physicians since the advent of the Medicare system in 1965. The fee schedule, which is based on a resource-based relative value scale (RBRVS), began in 1992 with full implementation on January 1, 1996.

Up until implementation of the Medicare RBRVS system in 1989, Medicare and commercial insurance payors established reimbursement to physicians based on "customary, prevailing, and reasonable charges." The system was criticized as inflationary and complex and as tending to retain distorted charges. Many physicians also criticized customary, prevailing, and reasonable payment rates as irrational, inequitable, and possibly leading to abuse. Under this system, each practice received annually a Medicare Profile that provided Medicare-allowed fees (the amount Medicare considered "allowable") for participating and nonparticipating physicians. The profile was adjusted annually based on the usual and customary rates for the geographic area and specialty. The allowed fee was based on a percentage of the actual charges submitted by all payors in a geographic area based on specialties. Consequently, as practices increased their fees, Medicare reimbursement likewise increased. If fees decreased, however, physicians would likely increase volume to offset any loss of revenue.

PARTICIPATION VERSUS NONPARTICIPATION

In the 1980s and early 1990s, participating with Medicare was not the norm, as the fees for nonparticipating physicians were greater than those of participating physicians. Nonparticipating physicians could choose on a case-by-case basis whether to accept assignment for services. If physicians accepted assignment, they would file a claim with Medicare and receive payment directly from Medicare; they still could bill the patient for the difference between the usual and customary fee and the amount received from Medicare. (This was known as balance billing.)

If physicians did not accept assignment, the patient would receive the full payment from Medicare and would in turn be responsible for paying physicians the amount billed, which would also be the usual and customary fee. The major difference for nonparticipating physicians would be whether to accept assignment. In general, accepting assignment meant receiving payment from Medicare directly, and collection activities were limited to the patient balance. Most practices were able to realize a higher collection percentage, lower billing expenses, and a higher dollar reimbursement by not participating in the program.

In 1987 Congress enacted legislation that placed limits on the amount nonparticipating physicians could charge Medicare patients. The physician population considered this legislation to be a move on the part of the government to force physicians into participating with Medicare as a means of controlling costs. Initially the disparity between the maximum allowable actual charge (MAAC; the limited fee established by HCFA) and physicians' usual and customary fees was such that most physicians were still not compelled to participate with the program. The Omnibus Budget Reconciliation Act (OBRA) of 1989 included new provisions regarding the MAAC charge calculations.

In 1991, with the implementation of the RBRVS fee schedule, the nomenclature for this fee limit was changed to "charge limits." Beginning January 1, 1991, the charge limit on unassigned claims by nonparticipating physicians could not exceed 125 percent of nonparticipating physicians' prevailing charge for most services. This difference was to be reduced in 1992 to 120 percent and for 1993 and subsequent years to 115 percent. A nonparticipating physician's allowed fee is set at 95 percent of that of a participating provider. As the disparity between the nonparticipating and participating physician fees decreased, the financial benefits of nonparticipation disappeared. Physicians who had never participated with the Medicare program felt they were forced into signing the participation agreement.

The national fee schedule (RBRVS) was established for two purposes:

1. Establish a uniform, logical basis for physician reimbursement.
2. Slow the rise in spending for physician services. Reimbursement from Medicare for physician services is governed by Part B of the Medicare statute.

Fees are established based on RBRVS, which takes into account five factors:

1. The time it takes for the typical physician to provide a service or perform a procedure
2. Difficulty of the effort (risk)
3. Geographic area and cost of living within the geographic area (GPCI, geographic practice cost index)
4. Practice overhead costs within the geographic areas
5. Cost of malpractice units

The relative value unit portion of RBRVS is comprised of the following three components:

1. PErvu: Practice expense RVU
2. Wrvu: Physician work RVU
3. Mrvu: Malpractice RVU

The actual payment to the physician (fee schedule amount) is calculated based on a formula that includes the RVUs and GPCI for an area. The result is multiplied by a conversion factor, an amount set by the Department of Health and Human Services and/or Congress, to arrive at an allowed amount for the service or procedure. The continued refinement and allocation of the factors above and related changes in the conversion factor have had a significant impact on medical practice reimbursement.

For example, the RBRVS conversion factor (CF) will increase for all physician services, except anesthesia, from $34.7315 in 1999 to $36.6137 in the year 2000. This represents a 5.4 percent physician fee increase. However, specialists who use their own clinical employees to treat patients in a hospital setting will realize a lower reimbursement in year 2000. The reduction in reimbursement is a result of the plan by the Health Care Financing Administration (HCFA) to reduce the practice expense (PE) portion of the RVUs for "facility" services (services that are not performed in the physician's office).

HCFA maintains that the Medicare Part A provisions which govern hospital reimbursement already include reimbursement for clinical staff to assist physicians in the hospital setting; therefore, the practice expense portion of the RVU should be lower for those services provided in the hospital. The corrections in computations for the practice expense portion of RBRVS have and continue to result in significant reductions for some specialists (1 to 8 percent reductions). The revisions are being phased in over a four year period, which began in 1999 and will be fully implemented in 2003.

MEDICAID

Medicaid, the federally funded, state-run program for the indigent, has historically reimbursed well below the median fee structure for all types of healthcare providers. The federal government provides general guidelines to the states for administration of these funds. Each state develops its own parameters for provider reimbursement. This information is available from the state insurance commissioner's office. Medicaid revenues average approximately 6 percent of group practice income.

MANAGED CARE/COMMERCIAL PAYORS

Although traditional healthcare indemnity policies are still available to beneficiaries, they do not control the market as they did before the mid-1990s. These plans are considered unmanaged and therefore have no control over costs. Reimbursement under indemnity plans basically includes a deductible and maximum out of pocket paid by the beneficiary with the balance being paid by the insurance company. Some readers will remember policies with provisions for a $200 deductible and 80 percent paid by insurance with 20 percent paid by the beneficiary.

Reimbursement methodology under these plans was based on the usual, customary, and prevailing fee structure. Some of the major insurance payors structured their fees on the McGraw-Hill Relative Values for Physicians methodology. Either way, physicians were basically paid at "retail." According to data from employer surveys in 1989 by the Health Insurance Association of America, these products represented 49 percent of the health insurance products sold in the United States. Individuals bore very little financial responsibility under this system.

In 1992, $830 billion or 14 percent of total economic output, was spent on healthcare. According to the July 1993 Congressional Budget Office Report, expenditures as a percentage of gross national product (GNP) rose from 6 percent to over 14 percent from 1965 to 1993. Although Medicare outlays for fiscal year 1999 decreased, first-quarter results for fiscal year 2000 reflect about a 2 percent increase over the same period for fiscal 1999. The Monthly Budget Review Fiscal Year 2000 (available on line at www.cbo.gov), states that year 2000 Medicaid spending is up 10 percent over the previous year. Following suit with the federal government, insurance companies during the 1990s looked for ways to restructure products that would keep premiums affordable and sustain profit margins. Cutting costs means reduction of services. Managed care products were added to the menu. Health maintenance organization enrollment grew from 15 million in 1983 to 70 million in 1999. Increase in HMO plans has meant a decrease in reimbursement to physicians with deeply discounted fee-for-service contracts for specialists and capitated payments for primary care physicians.

The total of the above (46 percent managed care, 22 percent Medicare, 6 percent Medicaid) equals 74 percent. The logical conclusion is that physicians have lost control of the "top line" (collections) since third parties control 74 percent of group practice revenues. MGMA *Cost Survey: 1999 Report* indicates that the median gross collection percentage for multispecialty practices declined from a high of 90.2 percent in 1982 to a low of 68.4 percent in 1998. Obviously, fee increases will no longer have a significant impact on the bottom line.

OVERHEAD TRENDS

As reimbursement continues to decline, costs continue to climb. Overhead or operating costs continue to increase as the marketplace becomes more complex. For example, median cardiology overhead that was 36.54% of collected revenue in 1992, based on the MGMA *Cost Survey: 1993 Report Based on 1992 Data*, increased to 42.88 percent in 1998 (MGMA *Cost Survey: 1999 Report Based on 1998 Data*). The 1999 report indicates an overall increase in operating costs for multispecialty practices of 54.0 percent in 1987 to 58.81 percent in 1998.

These percentages have been adjusted upward based on decreased revenues and increased expenses. The major expense category for a medical group is in personnel. Up until the 1990s, physicians could hire limited numbers of staff at not much more than minimum wage rates. The economic growth rate during the 1990s resulted in a tight labor market, which gave employees the leverage to ask for and receive higher starting salaries than previous years. Not only did salaries increase during this period, the need for additional staff increased due to the administrative requirements inherent in managed care contracts.

COMPETITION AND THE IMPACT ON PHYSICIAN COMPENSATION

Since the 1930s, physician compensation has benefited from the strict and limited entry into the profession. In the early 1900s, physicians earned little more than skilled laborers (approximately $750 per year, or $12,000 per year in today's dollars). Once they succeeded in establishing limited enrollment to medical schools and strict licensure requirements, physicians rose to the top of the professional salary ladder by 1930, with average annual earnings of $5,600 per year ($500 per year in excess of lawyers).

Now increased competition may be negatively affecting physician compensation. An article in the July 20, 1994, *Journal of the American Medical Association (JAMA)* predicted a surplus of certain specialties by the year 2000. The reality is that many specialties have experienced a decline in real income over the past decade (1987 to 1996). Cardiology, a specialty that was predicted to be oversupplied in a 1994 *JAMA* article, realized a 3 percent income decline in real dollars from 1987 to 1996.

Primary care physicians are likewise feeling the pinch of competition. The threat of healthcare reform in the early 1990s inspired many medical students to seek primary care residencies. The expectation was that the demand for specialists would decline under proposed reforms. Studies performed in the early 1990s indicated that there was an oversupply of subspecialists and an undersupply of primary care physicians. Studies performed in 1999 indicate that this trend has reversed and there is a shortage of specialists.

Initially, healthcare organizations heavily recruited primary care physicians to establish their "gatekeeper" base. Once the primary care network was established, however, the organizations rounded out their networks with specialists. Additionally, in highly managed care markets, midlevel providers (i.e., nurse practitioners, physician assistants) are being recruited in lieu of primary care physicians. The result is a decline in employment offers for primary care doctors completing their residency in 1999.

Increasing competition combined with panel requirements for managed care plans have likewise affected group practice income. Many specialists have felt the effects of closed panels, especially from major payors in an area.

DISEASE OF ME, DEFEAT OF US

The pie is shrinking and the table manners have changed. Physicians must be certain that they are being "fairly" compensated from the shrinking pool. Remaining chapters concern problems and challenges in the definition of "fair." In the context of compensation, "fair" typically equates to what is fair for each individual in the physician group. Thus fair is defined in the eyes of the beholder. The goal of the physician compensation model must be to establish a sense of fairness among the individual physicians while promoting group incentives.

CHAPTER THREE

Defining the Pie

No matter how thin you slice it, it's still baloney.
—Alfred E. Smith

The definition of what constitutes the revenue "pie" differs from practice to practice. Properly defining the shrinking pie is an important part of the compensation process. The "pie" forms the basis from which the revenue division will occur.

NET CASH AVAILABLE

The majority of group practices distribute bonus or incentive compensation from available cash. This definition of the pie holds some financial validity in that the practice cannot realistically pay out more in compensation than the cash on hand.

Timing of the incentive calculation becomes important in this scenario. Assume, for instance, that the calculation is based on financial results as of March 31. However, the bonus calculation is not complete until April 15. The bonus calculation typically is based on profits. Cash does not always equal profits. If the cash balance has declined since March 31, then the bonus distribution could be in excess of available cash. Therefore, the compensation pool to be divided must be defined based on the cash available at the time of distribution.

Additionally, it is important to include accounts payable in this scenario. Administrators/office managers may be tempted to delay the payment of accounts payable in order to increase the pie. Management also must consider other sources and uses of cash, such as the purchase of capital assets out of current period earnings (cash). Groups often make purchases throughout the year from available cash without determining the tax effect of the transactions. Typically when this occurs, the group will draw against a line of credit on the last day of the year in order to increase cash to the level of profit and pay out compensation to the physicians. Avoiding debt considerations is a dangerous practice that can result in serious financial implications to the group over time.

Another consideration or adjustment to the net cash available pie is that of reserving cash for working capital needs. Based on management information, a group may decide to provide a bonus of 50 percent of available cash during the year with 75 or 100 percent paid out annually or semiannually. This decision will vary group by group. Both tax and financial planning issues must be considered when deciding what funds are available to distribute.

NET INCOME

Groups also may use net income at the end of the calculation period to compute incentive pay. The advantage of using this method to define the pie is that it should reflect the financial results of the period being evaluated.

An important consideration in this method is the basis on which the financial statements are prepared. If they are on the cash basis (income tax basis), they may not reflect accounts payable. If they are on the accrual basis (Generally Accepted Accounting Principles), the methodology used to value accounts receivable (allowance for contractual adjustments and doubtful accounts) will have a significant impact on the bottom line.

In either basis of accounting, net income should be defined as either before physician compensation or after physician compensation. Physician compensation should be defined in terms of base salary or draw against total compensation plus those benefits and direct expenses that are included in compensation. Some groups include benefits in operating expenses, although this is not the norm.

Additionally, net income may be significantly different from the cash available. For instance, if the practice is servicing debt, the net income may very well exceed cash available. Net income may vary significantly from available cash based on increases in accounts receivable and investments in capital assets.

Depreciation can open up some interesting discussions. Many groups will choose not to record depreciation on a monthly basis if they are making principal payments toward the purchase of equipment. Their position is that depreciation reduces income and principal payments reduce cash, and therefore they have been "hit" twice for the same expense. Our experience has been that most physicians do not understand the concept of depreciation, and when the depreciation does not match the principal payments, the situation becomes more complicated. In general, as long as the compensation is sufficient to meet the individual's needs, depreciation is not a concern.

"EAT WHAT YOU KILL"

"Eat what you kill" describes the process of defining the pie in components and allocating the net results of each slice to individual physicians. In this scenario, each physician is credited with his or her share of collections and is allocated a share of practice expenses based on a predetermined formula. The net calculation forms the basis for the physician's total compensation pool.

The danger with this type of system lies in the incentive calculation. If the base salary is set too high, a physician may overdraw and actually be in a deficit rather than an incentive/bonus position. In a group setting, this situation may result in a bonus calculation for one physician while another physician has a deficit. It is imperative that the calculations be made at least quarterly in order to prevent discrepancies in the formula.

Example: Assume the group calculates incentives at year-end only. Physician A is due a bonus of $10,000 and Physician B has a deficit of $10,000. The practice, at this point, may have no cash to pay the bonus since Physician B basically has used up Physician A's bonus. In this situation, it is very difficult to extract the cash from Physician B to redistribute to Physician A. The tendency may be to carry the deficit forward and hope that the situation will be self-correcting while obtaining a loan to pay out Physician A.

Physician	A	B
Collections	$250,000	$300,000
Expenses (50/50)	125,000	125,000
Net Income Before Physician Compensation	$125,000	$175,000
Less Draws and Benefits	115,000	185,000
Net due to (from)	$10,000	$(10,000)
Cash available	$0	$0

Statistics are like a bikini. What they reveal is
suggestive, but what they conceal is vital.
—Aaron Lowenstein

BONUS VERSUS INCENTIVE

Definitions are extremely important in the design of the compensation system. It is not unusual to find that members within a group and of different groups have philosophical differences in how they perceive distributions in excess of base salary should be made. "Incentive" may be defined as a true motivation of working more or harder. "Bonus" may be defined as distributions over and above salary, benefits, and incentive pay.

A bonus may be a periodic distribution of profits over and above allocated incentive pools. The basis for distribution may be on ownership percentages, seniority, good citizenship, or any other basis the governing body deems appropriate and fair. This method of compensation often occurs when a capital partner participates in profits of the organization. Unless the bonus is to be treated as a dividend, care should be taken in the incorporated practice to tie the bonus to the personal service of the individual receiving the bonus.

Most closely owned groups will distribute all profits or available cash as incentive payments based on some definition of production. A properly designed incentive program can motivate and align individual behavior with group goals and strategies.

FINANCIAL REPORTING

The practice financial statements are the starting point for administration of the compensation plan. Regardless of the method of accounting, the format for financial statement presentation is best suited to that adopted by the American Institute of Certified Public Accountants for professional service organizations. Examples are included in the appendixes. This format is supported by the Chart of Accounts for Health Care Organizations as developed by the Center for Research in Ambulatory Health Care Administration, the research arm of the Medical Group Management Association.

Very few financial statements are the end product for distributing income. Most compensation plans require additional spreadsheet calculations. The dilemma is to prepare the information in a format that is easily understood and reflects the intent of the compensation plan and provides the pertinent data. (Pertinent data include that information that the physicians understand is the basis for allocation, charges, payments, RVUs, etc.) These issues will be discussed in depth as we consider the measurement of productivity in Chapter 11.

CHAPTER FOUR

Regulatory Considerations in Physician Compensation Arrangements

There is only one good, knowledge, and one evil, ignorance.
—Plato

Numerous regulatory requirements affect physician compensation models. Regulatory restrictions exist both at the federal and state level. State restrictions may include such regulations as the corporate practice of medicine, fee splitting, licensure laws, and insurance laws. Obviously, state rules vary from state to state. Federal considerations include compensation agreements for tax-exempt entities and tax-exempt financing, antitrust, fraud and abuse considerations, antikickback law, and the Stark laws which are addressed in this chapter.

Regulatory requirements regarding physician compensation are detailed, complex, and constantly changing. Only the highlights of current selected regulations are included in this text. Because the penalties for violations of these laws are so great, healthcare financial managers need to be aware of what conduct is prohibited and what conduct is permissible under the so-called safe harbors in order to protect their facility and its officers and practitioners from possible criminal or civil liability, including exclusion from all federal or federally funded health programs. Due to the serious implications of noncompliance, legal counsel may be recommended to determine the appropriateness of compensation arrangements effected under federal and state statutes.

TAX-EXEMPT ORGANIZATION

Physician compensation arrangements in tax-exempt organizations (those entities under section 501(c)(3) that are exempt from federal tax) must consider the issue of excess compensation in violation of the prohibition on private inurement. Tax-exempt entities must not allow their net earnings to inure to the benefit of any private person. Likewise, they must operate in a manner that serves the public interest. This means that any private benefit arising from the activity undertaken by the healthcare provider must be incidental to the public benefit. The public benefit requirement generally means that payments to private persons must not be in excess of fair market value.

The Internal Revenue Service (IRS) considers physicians to be insiders in transactions with tax-exempt health providers and will apply the private inurement restrictions to all transactions between the physician and the tax-exempt entity. Therefore, all transactions and compensation arrangements between physicians and tax-exempt healthcare providers are subject to a high degree of scrutiny to determine if the arrangement is, in fact, an arm's-length transaction and to ensure that compensation is not in excess of fair market value. Any payment received by the physician in excess of fair market value will constitute a form of private inurement.

The reasonableness of compensation paid to the physician is determined in light of the market. Comparable data regarding compensation amounts paid by institutions of similar size and location are used in making the determination. Surveys such as those conducted by the Medical Group Management Association along with actual offer letters from similar institutions may be used in establishing market compensation. Additionally, consideration is given to activities and responsibilities of the physician.

RECRUITMENT AGREEMENTS

It is not uncommon for a healthcare organization to offer financial assistance to physicians to assist with starting a practice in that organization's service area. Typical recruiting incentives include:

- Private practice income guarantees
- Assistance in financing the purchase of office equipment
- Assistance with student loan financing

In order for loans, income guarantees, or other subsidies not to violate the inurement prohibition, the healthcare provider must demonstrate two things:

1. That the incentive offered is incidental to the achievement of the tax-exempt healthcare provider's purpose of providing healthcare to the community
2. That the incentive paid constitutes reasonable compensation for the benefit conferred upon or services rendered for the benefit of the healthcare provider

The health provider must be able to establish that there is a need for the physician in the community served by the health provider in order to establish that the incentive furthers the charitable purposes of the provider. If there is no compelling need or a significant other benefit to the community, the arrangement with the physician should require full repayment at a reasonable rate of interest, with adequate security. In order to establish need, the healthcare provider should rely on objective evidence documenting the need. Objective data may include the absence of practitioners in a given specialty, studies of health manpower, and/or care provided to community members out of the service area.

Reasonableness for a recruiting incentive and/or compensation may be determined by examining the value of the physician's services to the healthcare provider, such as a new service or enhanced productivity, or the community, such as a needed specialty. Objective data such as comparable incentives or compensation paid for the type of practice and other physicians of the same level of experience should be used to document reasonableness.

The IRS will consider the following in determining whether a compensation arrangement violates the rules against inurement:

- Did an independent board or compensation committee set the compensation amount?
- Does the board have a substantial conflicts-of-interest policy (i.e., a policy that would prohibit a physician member from voting on matters related to that member's compensation)?
- Does the physician participate in management or control the healthcare organization in a way that affects the compensation arrangement?
- Is there a compensation ceiling to ensure a reasonable maximum amount of compensation in the event of windfall profits?

- Does the compensation arrangement have any provisions that would induce members to reduce the charitable services or benefits that the organization otherwise would provide?

- Is quality of care and patient satisfaction data taken into account in the compensation arrangement?

- If there is a sharing in net revenues, does the arrangement have the proper incentives in place to ensure that the organization's charitable purpose is accomplished?

- Does the compensation arrangement change the principal activity of the organization into a joint venture between it and the physician members?

- Is the compensation arrangement basically a device to distribute all or a portion of the healthcare organization's profits to physician members who are in control of the organization?

- Does the compensation arrangement have a real and discernible business purpose of the exempt organization?

- Does the compensation arrangement have effective controls to guard against unnecessary utilization, abuse, and/or unwarranted benefits?

- Does the compensation arrangement reward the physician based on services the physician actually performs or is it based on performance in an area where the physician performs no significant functions?

- Does the compensation arrangement result in total compensation that is reasonable based on the merits of each case?

Any subsidy for the private practice should be structured in such a manner as to require ultimate repayment in cash or in kind by the physician. The repayment may be satisfied by a requirement that the physician remain in the service area of the healthcare provider for a period of time after the end of the benefit period and accept patients during such period irrespective of their ability to pay. Likewise, the benefit provided to the physician should be fully reported on the appropriate forms (1099) to the IRS, including any imputed interest or the reduced cost for the use of services and/or facilities.

TAX-EXEMPT FINANCING

Any entity obtaining tax-exempt financing or that has tax-exempt financing contracts with an entity that is not tax-exempt must follow Revenue

Procedure (Rev. Proc.) 97–13 issued by the Internal Revenue Service. Although a revenue procedure does not constitute law, the bond counsel of tax-exempt healthcare enterprise usually requires it to comply with its guidelines before issuing tax-exempt debt.

Rev. Proc. 97–13 applies to all management contracts between any governmental or 501(c)(3) tax-exempt healthcare organization entered into or materially modified after May 16, 1997. The definition of the term "management contracts" includes "an incentive payment contract for physician services to patients of a hospital." Compensation restrictions are specifically stated in Rev. Proc. 93–19. Appendix D of this book includes a copy. In general, any service contract with an entity that has issued tax-exempt bonds must provide for reasonable compensation in exchange for services actually rendered. The contract must not provide for any compensation for services based, in whole or in part, on a share of "net profits from the operation" of the facility. For purposes of this revenue procedure, "net profits from the operation" does not include productivity rewards equal to a stated dollar amount based on increases or decreases in gross revenues (or adjusted gross revenues), or reductions in total expenses (but not both increases in gross revenues or adjusted gross revenues and reductions in total expenses) in any annual period during the term of the contract. Generally, these arrangements do not cause the compensation to be based on a share of net profits.

Rev. Proc. 97–13 has been interpreted as an IRS blessing on "gain-sharing" arrangements. In response, the Office of the Inspector General (OIG) issued a Special Advisory Bulletin dated July 8, 1999, regarding gain-sharing arrangements. "Gain-sharing" refers to an arrangement in which a hospital gives physicians financial rewards for helping to reduce the hospital's costs for patient care. The advisory bulletin advises hospitals and physicians that the civil money penalty (CMP) law prohibits hospitals knowingly from paying physicians directly or indirectly as an inducement to reduce or limit services to Medicare or Medicaid beneficiaries under the physicians' care (Social Security Act 1128A[b][1]). The bulletin also indicates that such arrangements may violate the antikickback statute and the Stark self-referral laws and would be subject to civil money penalties. Penalties are imposed up to $2,000 per patient. Legal opinion is recommended in developing any hospital physician compensation arrangement.

In addition to the civil money penalties just discussed, violation of Rev. Proc. 93-19 results in the revocation of tax exemption of the interest paid to the bondholders, which in turn results in the bonds becoming immediately payable.

FRAUD AND ABUSE

> *If fifty million people say a foolish thing, it is still a foolish thing.*
> —Anatole France

Federal "fraud and abuse" law is actually a compilation of several laws, including the federal antikickback law, the federal self-referral ban (Stark I and II), federal Medicare and Medicaid false claims laws, and other federal payor program antikickback provisions (such as CHAMPUS).

ANTIKICKBACK STATUTE

The antikickback law prohibits any payments to induce referrals. According to the OIG in a February 2000 Special Fraud Alert, "Kickbacks can distort medical decision making, cause overutilization, increase costs and result in unfair competition by freezing out competitors who are unwilling to pay kickbacks. Kickbacks can also adversely affect the quality of patient care by encouraging physicians to order services or recommend supplies based on profit rather than the patients' best medical interests."

The fraud and abuse statutory regulation that applies to physician compensation is found at 42 U.S.C. 1320a-7b(b), which states:

> Whoever knowingly and willfully offers or pays any remuneration (including any kick back, bribe, or rebate) directly or indirectly, overtly or covertly, in cash or in kind to any person to induce such person . . . to refer an individual to a person for the furnishing or arranging for the furnishing of any item or service for which payment may be made in whole or in part under [the Medicare Program] for a State health care program shall be guilty of a felony and upon conviction thereof shall be fined not more than $25,000 or imprisoned for not more than five (5) years, or both.

In addition, a conviction under this statute mandates exclusion from the Medicare and Medicaid program, according to 42 U.S.C. 1320a-7(a),7(b)(7).

In order for remuneration to exist, there must be some tangible incentive provided. Although cash is the most likely incentive for a physician practice, remuneration broadly stated in the statue also may include forgiveness of debt, below-market rent, and the like. A referral includes business in any form, including but not limited to direct patient care services, diagnostic tests, and/or equipment.

It is important to note that a referral does not actually have to occur in order to violate this statute. If remuneration is made to a person who is in a position to make a referral, a violation may be deemed regardless of whether an actual referral occurred.

In order to violate this statute, the participants in the transaction must act "knowingly and willfully." In other words, the participants must have intentionally entered into a prohibited transaction.

The Department of Health and Human Services and the OIG have established safe harbors to protect by regulation certain payment practices that may have contained the elements for a violation of the Fraud and Abuse Statute but that clearly were not intended to be prohibited. The initial safe harbors issued on July 29, 1991, that relate to physician compensation arrangements include the following:

1. Personal services and management contracts: This safe harbor is intended to protect legitimate arrangements in which a physician is in a position to refer but is providing services and is receiving only fair market compensation for those services. In order to be effective, the arrangement must be in writing and must specify the services to be provided. Additionally, the term of the agreement must not be for less than one year. The aggregate compensation paid over the term of the agreement must be set in advance and must be consistent with fair market values and must not take into account the volume or value of any referrals or business otherwise generated between the parties.

2. Employees: All payments made as part of a legitimate employment relationship are protected. Protected payments include those payments made by an employer to an employee who has a bona fide employee relationship. The definition for employee in this safe harbor has the same requirements as the 20 factor test set forth in the Internal Revenue Code.

3. Sale of a practice: Certain payments made as part of a practitioner's acquisition of another physician's medical practice are protected. This safe harbor does not apply to acquisitions of medical practices by hospitals. In order to be protected by this safe harbor, the period from the date of the first agreement pertaining to the sale to the completion of the sale must not be more than one year. Additionally, the practitioner who is selling his or her practice must not be in a professional position to make referrals to the purchasing practitioner.

4. Space and equipment rental: The legitimate receipt of rental payments for equipment or office space is protected by this safe harbor.

In order to be protected, the lease must be in writing specifying the equipment or location covered by the lease. The term of the agreement must be for at least one year, and the lease amount must be consistent with fair market value. The lease amount may not take into account the volume or value of any referrals or business otherwise generated between the parties.

5. Investment interests: This safe harbor addresses both investment interests in large, publicly traded companies and investments in smaller companies (i.e., integrated delivery providers with physician ownership). Protected under this safe harbor are payments and profit distributions that are only minimally related to referral patterns. In order to be protected, no more than 40 percent of the value of the investment interests of each class of investors may be held in the previous year by investors who are in a position to make or influence referrals. The investment interest must be offered on the same terms to all passive investors. The entity or any investor must not market or furnish the entity's items or services to passive investors differently than to non-investors. No more than 40 percent of the gross revenue of the entity in the previous year may come from referrals or business generated from investors. The entity must not loan funds to or guarantee a loan for an investor who is in a position to make or influence referrals if any part of the loan is used to obtain the investment interest. Last, the amount of a payment to an investor in return for the investment interest must be directly proportional to the amount of the capital investment of that investor.

In the November 19, 1999 *Federal Register*, the OIG issued its codification of eight new safe harbors. Four are designed to encourage delivery of medical services in "medically underserved areas" (MUAs) and "health professional shortage areas" (HSPAs).

These four safe harbors are as follows:

1. Joint ventures: In underserved areas, the agency will permit a 50 percent ownership by physicians in a position to refer (increased above the existing safe harbor rate of 40 percent). At least 75 percent of the venture's patients must be from a medically underserved area.

2. Physician recruitment: Entities may make payments to physicians to attract them to MUAs, if at least 75 percent of the recruited practitioner's revenue is from patients who live in underserved areas. The

safe harbor limits the term of incentive payments to three years. There is no distance requirement for relocation. Essentially, a physician can move from one underserved area in a city to another underserved area and still fulfill the requirements of this safe harbor. Additionally, there is no dollar limit on recruitment packages as long as the compensation is not contingent on referrals.

3. Sales of physician practices to hospitals: A hospital in an MUA may buy and hold the practice (i.e., patients) of a retiring physician until it recruits a new physician. The hospital must make a good-faith effort to find a new practice owner and must complete the sale within three years.

4. Subsidies for obstetrical malpractice insurance: Hospitals in underserved areas may pay all or part of the malpractice insurance for obstetricians they recruit. To qualify, at least 75 percent of the obstetric patients must live in a MUA.

Safe harbors for four types of investments in ambulatory surgery centers (ASC) are codified in the fifth safe harbor. The following entities may receive safe harbor protection if they meet detailed requirements:

- Surgeon-owned ASCs
- Single-specialty ASCs
- Multispecialty ASCs
- Hospital-physician–owned ASCs

Certain requirements apply to all four categories. First, the ASC must be Medicare-certified, and neither the ASC nor the physician investors can discriminate against federal program beneficiaries. Additionally, physician investors are required to inform any patient they refer to the ASC about their investment interest. All ancillary services must be an integral part of the procedures performed at the ASC and cannot be billed separately. Loans from the ASC or other investors for the purpose of investing are prohibited, and investment interests cannot be based on the volume or value of referrals.

In the first three financial arrangements, surgeon owners must perform at least one-third of their ASC services in the ASC they own. Physicians and group practices may own part of the ASC, provided they do not send referrals or qualify for another safe harbor. Hospitals with investment interests must not be in a position to refer patients to the ASC.

Other safe harbors that relate to physician compensation arrangements include:

- Investments in group practices: Physicians may invest in their own group practices if the group practice meets the Stark law's definition of a group practice.

- Specialty referral arrangements: This permits referrals from a general practitioner to a surgeon with the provision that the surgeon will refer the patient back to the general practitioner for follow-up visits. This safe harbor does not protect splitting a global fee from Medicare. The referrals must be medically necessary and must not be on a forced timetable.

The OIG also attempted to clarify six of the original 11 safe harbors created in 1991. Specifically, the OIG's rule covers the existing safe harbors pertaining to large- and small-entity investments, space rental, equipment rental, and personal services and management contracts, referral services, and discounts.

With regard to space and equipment rental and personal services and management contracts, the OIG stated that it will apply a new "commercially reasonable business" test to determine whether a particular arrangement is protected under any of these safe harbors. Under this standard, the OIG advises that the "rental or purchase must be of space, equipment, or services that the lessee or purchaser needs, intends to utilize and does utilize in furtherance of its commercially reasonable business objectives." The OIG states that this test does not depend on whether the business arrangement is lawful but on whether the space and equipment leased or services purchased have "intrinsic commercial value" to the lessee or purchaser.

The OIG's February 2000 Special Fraud Alert identified three questionable features of suspect rental arrangements for space in physicians' offices. The three areas are:

1. The appropriateness of rental agreements: The threshold inquiry when examining rental payments is whether payment for rent is appropriate at all. Payments of "rent" for space that traditionally has been provided for free or for a nominal charge as an accommodation between the parties for the benefit of the physicians' patients, such as consignment closets for durable medical equipment, may be disguised kickbacks. In general, payments for rent of consignment closets in physicians' offices are suspect.

2. Rental amounts: Rental amounts should be at fair market value, be fixed in advance, and not take into account, directly or indirectly, the volume or value of referrals or other business generated between the parties. Fair market value rental payments should not exceed the

amount paid for comparable property. When a physician rents space, the rate paid by the supplier should not exceed the rate paid by the physicians, in the primary lease for the office space, except in rare circumstances. Examples of suspect rentals include:

- Rental amounts in excess of amounts paid for comparable property rented in arm's-length transactions between persons not in a position to refer business
- Rental amounts for subleases that exceed the rental amounts per square foot in the primary lease
- Rental amounts that are subject to modification more often than annually
- Rental amounts that vary with the number of patients or referrals
- Rental arrangements that set a fixed rental fee per hour but do not fix the number of hours or the schedule of usage in advance
- Rental amounts that are paid only if there are a certain number of federal healthcare program beneficiaries referred each month
- Rental amounts that are conditioned on the supplier's receipt of payments from a federal healthcare program

3. Time and space considerations: Suppliers should only rent premises of a size and for a time that is reasonable and necessary for a commercially reasonable business purpose of the supplier. Rental of space that is in excess of suppliers' need creates a presumption that the payments may be a pretext for giving money to physicians for their referrals. Examples of suspect arrangements include:

- Rental amounts for space that is unnecessary or not used. For instance, an entity requires one examination room and rents physician office space one afternoon a week when the physician is not in the office. The entity calculates its rental payment on the square footage for the entire office, since it is the only occupant during that time, even though the lessee needs only one examination room.
- Rental amounts for time when the rented space is not in use by the supplier. For example, an ultrasound supplier has enough business to support the use of one examination room for four hours each week, but rents the space for an amount equivalent to eight hours per week.
- Nonexclusive occupancy of the rented portion of space. For example, a physical therapist does not rent space in a physician's office but rather moves from examination room to examination

room treating patients after they have been seen by the physician. Since no particular space is rented, the OIG will closely scrutinize the pro-ration of time and space used to calculate the therapist's "rent."

Rental calculations should pro-rate the rent based on the amount of space and duration of time the premises are used. The basis for any pro-ration should be documented and updated as necessary. Depending on the circumstances, the supplier's rent can consist of three components:

1. Exclusive office space: The supplier's rent should be calculated based on the ratio of the time the space is in use by the supplier to the total amount of time the physician's office is in use. In addition, the rent should be calculated based on the ratio for the amount of space that is used exclusively by the supplier to the total amount of space in the physician's office. For example, where a supplier rents an examination room for four hours one afternoon per week in a physician's office that has four examination rooms of equal size and is open eight hours a day, five days per week, the supplier's pro-rated annual rent would be calculated as follows:

   Physician office rent per day × % of office space
   rented by supplier × % of each day rented by supplier
   × number of days rented by supplier per year
   = supplier's annual rent for exclusive space

2. Interior office common space: When permitted by applicable regulations, rental payments also may cover the interior office common space in physicians' offices that are shared by the physicians and any subtenants, such as waiting rooms. If suppliers use such common areas for their patients, it may be appropriate for the suppliers to pay a pro-rated portion of the charge for such space. The charge for the common space must be apportioned among all physicians and subtenants that use the interior office common space based on the amount of noncommon space they occupy and the duration of such occupation. Payment for the use of office common space should not exceed the supplier's pro rata share of the charge for such space based on the ratio of the space used exclusively by the supplier to the total amount of space (other than common space occupied by all persons using such common space.

3. Building commons space: Where the physician pays a separate charge for areas of a building that are shared by all tenants, such as

building lobbies, it may be appropriate for the supplier to pay a pro-rated portion of such charge. As with interior office common space, the cost of the building common space must be apportioned among all physicians and subtenants based on the amount of noncommon space they occupy and the duration of such occupation.

In order to qualify for a safe harbor, the arrangement must fit squarely into the safe harbor. The OIG commented that arrangements not falling specifically into a safe harbor would be reviewed on a case-by-case basis to determine compliance with antikickback statutes. Providers who are uncertain as to whether their arrangements qualify for safe harbor protection may request an advisory opinion, according to the OIG.

It is important to note that the Balanced Budget Act of 1997 added "bite" to the antikickback statute by extending the violations to include civil money penalties of $50,000 for each violation. If the government cannot get you on the criminal side, it can go after you on the civil side. It is also important to note that meeting a safe harbor for the antikickback statute does not indicate that an arrangement would be in compliance with the Stark laws.

STARK I AND STARK II

The Stark laws (Stark I and Stark II) often are referred to as the antireferral laws or the physician self-referral laws. The basic premise of both Stark laws is to discourage inappropriate ancillary referrals that result in a financial reward to the physician making the referral. Prior to the passage of the Stark laws, studies by the General Accounting Office (GAO) determined that physicians were ordering tests at a higher frequency when they maintained a financial interest in the entity providing the services. For example, a 1992 study found that at least 40 percent of the doctors in Florida who see patients directly referred them routinely to entities in which they had a financial interest.

The original Stark law (Stark I) was included in the Omnibus Budget Reconciliation Act of 1989 and prohibited a physician from referring a patient or specimens for Medicare-reimbursable services to a clinical laboratory participating in the Medicare program, if the physician (or an immediate family member of the physician) had a financial relationship (ownership interest or compensation arrangement) with the clinical laboratory provider. Further, clinical laboratories were prohibited from submitting claims or billing for reimbursement if the services were rendered in connection with a prohibited referral. The Stark I regulations were published in interim final form on August 14, 1995. The final Stark I regulations became effective on September 13, 1995.

Stark II became effective January 1, 1995, and expanded the scope of the referral prohibitions to all "designated health services" and added patients in the Medicaid program. Proposed regulations (400 pages) were issued for Stark II on January 8, 1998. Final regulations are estimated to be issued in June of year 2000. HCFA has publicly stated that a "good faith reasonable interpretation" of the Stark I and Stark II laws, in areas not covered by regulations already in effect, would not likely result in the finding of a violation. However, HCFA also has indicated that a referral in connection with a financial arrangement that fails to meet an exception is prohibited, even if unintentional. In February 2000 JoAnne Sinsheimer, HCFA lead drafter of the regulations, indicated that the final regulations will be drastically different from the proposed regulations. Ms. Sinsheimer specifically stated that one area in which the language would be reworked from the original regulations was compensation. She went on to say that HCFA will likely mandate enforcement of Stark prospectively, rather than retroactively, when final rules are issued.

The statement of prohibition under Stark states the following: If a physician (or immediate family member) has a *financial relationship* with an entity, the physician may not make a *referral* to that entity for the furnishing of *designated health services* for which payment may be made under the government programs, and the entity may not present or cause to be presented a claim to any individual, third-party payor, or other entity for designated health services furnished pursuant to a prohibited referral.

"Immediate family" is defined as husband or wife; natural or adoptive parent, child, or sibling; stepparent, stepchild, stepbrother, stepsister; father-in-law, mother-in-law, son-in-law, daughter-in-law, brother-in-law, sister-in-law; grandparent, grandchild, or spouse of a grandparent or grandchild.

The Stark laws define "financial relationship" to mean an ownership or investment interest in the entity or a compensation arrangement between the physician (or immediate family member) and the entity. Ownership can be constituted through equity, debt, or other means. "Compensation" is defined as any arrangement involving remuneration, either direct or indirect. "Remuneration" is broadly defined as anything of value, including discounts, forgiveness of debt, or other benefits made directly or indirectly, in cash or in kind. A financial arrangement therefore includes two distinct components: (1) ownership and (2) compensation.

A referral to a designated health service is constituted by a physician's request for the item or service for which payment may be made under Part B, including a request for a consultation with another physician and any tests or services ordered by the consulting physician. Moreover, a referral includes the request or establishment of a plan of care that calls for the provision of designated health services. The exception to the referral provision occurs when a consultation is requested by a radiologist, radiology oncologist, or pathologist. Referrals within a group practice include the ordering of any one physician for any designated health service, whether provided by the group practice or by an outside entity. For example, an oncologist orders chemotherapy treatment for a patient and such treatment is provided in the group practice office suite. The chemotherapy drugs and supplies are considered designated health services under the outpatient prescription drug provisions, and therefore the revenue generated from these drugs and/or supplies cannot be included directly in the individual physician's compensation.

The current list of designated health services as defined in the statute include:

- Clinical laboratory services
- Physical therapy services
- Occupational therapy services
- Radiology services, including magnetic resonance imaging (MRI), computerized axial tomography (CAT) scans, and ultrasound services
- Radiation therapy services and supplies
- Durable medical equipment and supplies
- Parenteral and enteral nutrients, equipment, and supplies
- Prosthetics, orthotics, and prosthetic devices and supplies
- Home health services
- Outpatient prescription drugs
- Inpatient and outpatient hospital services

Defining what constitutes a designated health service for Medicaid purposes is complicated by the fact that the coverage varies from Medicare and likewise varies from state to state. When the definition of a designated health service differs under a state's plan from the definition under Medicare, the state's plan definition should take precedence even if the definition encompasses services that are not covered by Medicare. However, Medicaid services will not be included in situations in which including those services appears to run counter to the underlying purpose of the Stark legislation.

Clarifications and examples of designated health services have been included in the *Federal Register*. They include, but are not limited to, the following:

- Physical therapy services include speech pathology services.
- Radiology includes interpreting MRIs, CAT scans, ultrasound, and radiation therapy and supplies.
- Screening mammography is excluded from the definition of designated health services.
- Radiology includes the physician's professional services.
- Invasive radiology is excluded from the definition of radiology. Invasive radiology includes any procedure in which the imaging modality is used to guide a needle, probe, or a catheter accurately.
- External infusion pumps used in a physician's office are covered under the "incident to" benefit and are not considered to be durable medical equipment.
- Holter monitoring is a diagnostic service and is not considered to be a designated health service.
- Parenteral and enteral nutrition are excluded from qualifying under the in-office ancillary exception.
- Prosthetics, orthotics, and prosthetic devices do not include diabetic shoes, casts, splints, or other devices used for the reduction of fractures and dislocations. This category does include pacemakers, intraocular lens implants (unless included in payment to an ambulatory surgery center), cochlear implants, and incontinence control appliances.
- Outpatient prescription drugs include oncology drugs that are routinely furnished in a physician's office, under the physician's direct supervision, provided the drugs could be obtained by prescription from a pharmacy; biologicals and vaccines also are included. Pharmaceuticals (such as EPO) for maintenance dialysis patients are excluded, as are dialysis services.
- Hospital inpatient services include services in psychiatric hospitals and in rural facilities.

Congress and the Office of the Inspector General and Human Services have created a number of exceptions to the Stark II statute. Exceptions include exemptions for bona fide employment relationships, personal service contracts, and space and equipment leases that meet a variety of requirements.

Exceptions to both ownership and compensation arrangements include:

- Services performed personally by, or under the personal supervision of, another physician in the same group practice as the referring physician.
- Certain services provided ancillary to the physician's or group's own professional services (in-office ancillary exception).
- Services provided by a federally qualified HMO or prepaid health plan with a contract with Medicare.
- Other financial relationships the secretary may determine pose no risk of patient or Medicare program abuse.

Exceptions to the ownership or investment prohibition include:

- Ownership of investment securities in publicly traded corporations with either total assets of $100 million prior to January 1, 1995, or equity exceeding $75 million at the end of the corporation's most recent fiscal year or on average for the past three years
- Ownership of shares in a regulated investment company that has total assets exceeding $75 million at the end of the corporation's most recent fiscal year or on average for the past three years
- Ownership or interest in rural providers if substantially all of the services are rendered to persons residing in the rural area; and interest in hospitals located in Puerto Rico
- Ownership or investment interests in a hospital as a whole if the physician has referring privileges to that hospital

Exceptions to the compensation arrangements include:

- Lease arrangements for office space or equipment if certain conditions are met; for instance, a written agreement for at least one year signed by the parties and payments that are for fair market value and not based on the volume or value of referrals
- Bona fide employment relationships where the requirements are similar to the lease arrangements
- Personal service arrangements, such as compensation, where the requirements are similar to the lease and employment arrangements, may not be determined in a manner that takes into account the volume or value of referrals

- Remuneration paid by an entity to a physician if the remuneration is not related to the provision of designated health services
- Recruitment arrangements where the physician is relocating to the hospital's geographic area and is not required to refer patients to the hospital
- Isolated financial transactions, such as the one-time sale of a property or practice where there is no continuing financing relationship between the physician and the entity
- Arrangements that began before December 19, 1989, whereby a group practice provides substantially all of the designated health services required by the hospital under arrangements
- Payments made by a physician to a laboratory for services rendered or made by a physician to an entity as compensation for items or services furnished at fair market value

Typically medical practices must make use of the in-office ancillary exception to protect referrals within the group practice of Medicare and Medicaid patients for designated health services.

In order to comply with the in-office ancillary service exception, the services must be furnished personally by the referring physician, a member of the same group practice, or an employee who is directly supervised by the ordering physician or a member of that physician's group practice. Additionally, the service must be furnished either in a building in which the referring physician or a member of that physician's group practice provides services other that the designated health services or in another building that is used by the practice for the centralized provision of the group's designated health services.

The law and proposed regulations also set out criteria that must be met to qualify as a group practice. A group is defined as two or more physicians, legally organized as a partnership, professional corporation, foundation, not-for-profit corporation, faculty practice plan, or similar association. Additionally, the practice must be a "unified business" with centralized decision making, pooling of expenses and revenues, and a compensation/profit distribution system that is not based on satellite offices operating as if they were separate enterprises or profit centers. Each physician who is a member of the group must furnish substantially the full range of services that the physician would routinely furnish in the group practice. Additionally, the physicians who constitute the group must, as a whole, perform "substantially all" of their services through the group practice. The term "substantially all" has been defined to equal 75 percent of the services performed by the members of the group.

Once these exception hurdles have been met, Stark imposes a further limitation. A group practice must not compensate its members based on their referrals of Medicare and Medicaid patients for designated health services. The typical practice of dividing income based on an individual physician's production (including designated health services) will expose the group and its members to the serious sanctions and penalties. A physician may be paid shares of overall profits of the group, provided the formula for determining profit sharing is predetermined. The compensation model can allow for a productivity bonus based on services personally performed as long as the bonus is not determined in a manner that relates to the volume of referrals. The volume and value of referrals cannot be reflected in the physician members' compensation.

The group's method for treating revenue and expense must reflect centralized decision making. Revenue and expenses must be pooled and may not be distributed based on satellite offices operating as if they were separate entities.

Effective systems under Stark include carve-outs of designated health services into separate revenue/cost centers. All income received and expenses incurred in relation to designated health services should be segregated and must be divided by the physicians on some basis not directly tied to referrals. Referrals are defined as "ordering" of those services and the services are not personally performed by the physician.

The simplest approach is to divide net income from designated health services equally among the physician members in the group. An equal division can, however, greatly distort compensation for multispecialty groups. As in a previous example, assume a family practice group merges with a surgical group. An equal allocation between all physicians of laboratory and radiology revenues, conceivably generated totally by family practice patients, could cause a significant shift in income out of the family practice compensation pool into the surgeons' pool. In some cases, the reallocation of designated health service income can cause such dramatic shifts that groups either disband or make a conscious decision not to comply.

In the example shown in Exhibit 4.1, by sharing net ancillary income equally, the family practice compensation pool was decreased by $45,000 and the surgeons picked up a windfall of $45,000. Obviously this is a very simple example; however, it points out the overall dilemma of sharing ancillary service revenue in a group practice.

Single-specialty groups must deal with the same issues. As long as all physicians are performing a fairly equal amount of designated health services, an equal sharing methodology probably will be acceptable. Once any one or more members of the group change their practice patterns by

EXHIBIT 4.1
Stark Implications

Net Income: Premerger		
	Family Practice	**Surgeon**
Collections—Professional Fees	$500,000	$1,100,000
Operating Expenses	200,000 (40%)	330,000 (30%)
Net Income Before Physician Compensation		
Professional Services	$300,000	$770,000
Collections—Ancillaries	$250,000	$100,000
Operating Expenses	$100,000 (40%)	$40,000 (40%)
Net Income Before Physician Compensation		
Ancillary Services	$150,000	$60,000
Total		
Net Income Before Physician Compensation		
(Physician Compensation Pool)	$450,000	$830,000

Net Income: Postmerger—Stark Ancillary Allocation		
	Family Practice	**Surgeon**
Collections—Professional Fees	$500,000	$1,100,000
Operating Expenses	200,000 (40%)	330,000 (30%)
Net Income Before Physician Compensation		
Professional Services	$300,000	$770,000
Collections—Ancillaries	$250,000	$100,000
Operating Expenses	$100,000 (40%)	$40,000 (40%)
Net Income Before Physician Compensation		
Ancillary Services	$150,000	$60,000
Total net ancillary income	$210,000	
Reallocate net evenly	$105,000	$105,000
Total		
Net Income Before Physician Compensation		
(Physician Compensation Pool)	$405,000	$875,000

either reducing time in the office or increasing their patient load, the perceived "fairness" of equal sharing becomes less evident. An example would be a group of oncologists providing chemotherapy treatment in their office suite.

Some physicians have a larger patient base that requires more office visits and less chemotherapy. Some physicians have a patient base that requires more chemotherapy services and fewer hospital or office visits. Patients presenting with different diseases will be treated differently. Additionally, physicians may choose different treatment plans requiring more or less expensive drugs. Some physicians in the group may decide to refer their patients to a "cancer center" and not supervise the chemo treatment. Any one of these issues may contribute to disparity in revenues that spark discord when determining how to share in those revenues. The point with Stark is that the basis for sharing these revenues should not be viewed as an incentive to "overutilize" the designated health service.

The consequences for noncompliance are serious and may be costly. The penalties are imposed even if the noncompliant act is unintentional. If a group practice is found to have a compensation model that is not in compliance with Stark, the practice can be penalized up to $100,000 per noncompliant agreement, plus up to three times the amount paid on claims submitted under the arrangement. Additionally, the practice (and the physician members) can be excluded from participation in the Medicare and Medicaid program. Other sanctions include:

- Denial of payment: Medicare will deny payment for services rendered in violation of Stark.
- Refunds: If a provider collects on a bill for a service that was in violation of Stark, the provider must refund the money within 60 days.

One of the clear themes emerging from the proposed regulations for Stark II that were issued on January 9, 1998, is that the range of compensation arrangements meeting exceptions under Stark II would be broadened, largely because new, expanded compensation exceptions are being proposed. HCFA has proposed three new exceptions:

1. Fair market value compensation exception
2. De minimis compensation exception
3. Discount exception

Other methods of allocating these revenues will be considered in Chapter 11.

FAIR MARKET VALUE COMPENSATION

The most important new provision in the proposed regulations addresses the most obvious omission in the original legislation, that of a "reasonableness" exception. Previously, if a physician's financial relationship with an entity did not fit neatly into one of a handful of specific statutory exceptions, then the physician could not refer Medicare patients to the entity for designated health services. Numerous common, nonabusive financial relationships do not meet any statutory exception.

The proposed new exception would protect any commercially reasonable business transaction between a physician and an entity that furthers legitimate business purposes if it meets certain minimum standards:

- The agreement must be in writing and must be signed by all parties.
- The agreement must include the specific items and services to be provided.
- The specific time frame for the arrangement must be specified. (If less than a year it cannot be altered more often than annually).
- The agreement must provide for fair market value compensation.
- The agreement must not take into account the volume or value of referrals or other business generated between the parties.
- The agreement must not violate the antikickback statute.

HCFA has specifically advised healthcare providers to make use of this new exception if an arrangement does not meet any other exception. The preamble to this exception states that parties "involved in a compensation arrangement should . . . use this exception if they have any doubts about whether they meet the requirements in other exception." If the proposed regulations become final with this new exception, Stark II will become much simpler to interpret and will accommodate the vast majority of nonabusive compensation arrangements between physicians and the entities to which they refer.

DE MINIMIS COMPENSATION

Another frustrating aspect of the Stark II legislation is its failure to provide any exception for de minimis compensation arrangements. This failure can bring into question everything from free coffee to free malpractice insurance. The proposed regulations provide some guidance through the inclusion of a de minimis compensation arrangement exception. The exception would protect compensation from an entity to a physician in the form of items or services (not including cash or cash equivalents) not exceeding $50 per gift or $300 per year, if the gift is provided to all similarly situated individuals, regardless of referrals, and if the compensation does not take account of the volume or value of referrals.

Although this exception will provide useful guidance in some situations, it also may create difficulties for entities that have what they consider to be de minimis compensation arrangements with a value in excess of $300 per year. For example, assume an entity provides free parking; however, the fair market value of the parking exceeds $300 per year. Should the facility begin charging the physician for the excess value? Obviously, doing so may cause additional administrative problems.

DISCOUNTS

This exception protects "any discount made to a physician that is passed on in full to either the patient or the patient's insurers (including Medicare) and that does not enure to the benefit of the referring physician." The purpose of this proposed exception is to protect discounts that "flow through" the physician from the person or entity providing the discount to the person or entity paying the physician for the discounted item or service. The rationale for this exception is that because the physician obtains no financial benefit from a discount that is passed on, through the physician, from the person selling to the physician to the person buying from the physician, the physician would have no financial incentive to steer referrals to the entity providing the discount.

There is some question as to why this exception would be necessary. Typically, the arrangement pursuant to which the person or entity is selling goods or services to the physician should qualify for an exception on its own terms because the payment terms under such an arrangement should be consistent with the fair market value of the goods and services provided to the physician, and an exception protects a physician's purchase of items at fair market value.

This exception, however, may provide additional comfort to those selling items or services to physicians at discounts that are so great that they might call into question whether their arrangements with physicians are consistent with fair market value. On the other hand, physicians who wish to mark up items or services that they have purchased at a discount may now be less comfortable relying on the exception that protects a physician's purchase of items or services at fair market value.

The proposed regulations provide additional exceptions; however, a central theme is evident in each proposal. The physician may not be compensated on the value or volume of referrals. Obviously, this creates a hurdle in group practice compensation design. The practice must meet an exception while subsequently designing a compensation system that is not related to the value or volume of referrals.

Designing compensation systems for both existing group practices and merging practices in compliance with Stark requires careful planning. Appropriate allocation of overhead becomes increasingly important. Additionally, the practice must consider carefully all the factors to be included in the model to ensure that group goals are achieved while maintaining compliance with Stark.

The House Ways and Means subcommittee has recognized the complicated nature of the Stark laws and the problems that this has caused to physician suppliers of healthcare services. Final regulations for Stark II have been in process for six years, with 16 exceptions and 12,000 comments. The subcommittee recognized the following problems in a hearing May 13, 1999, before the Office of the Inspector General and the Health Care Financing Committee:

- Stark hinders hospitals from creating new relationships that are intended to treat patients and improve care.
- HCFA's regulatory approach of closing loopholes and carving out exceptions will never keep up with advances in medical practices or with clever practitioners bent on circumventing the rules.
- The compensation restrictions are a source of problems. They demand perfection and create a harassing structure. These provisions require judgment on the propriety of arrangements on a graduated scale.
- Stark II prevents rural areas from getting needed equipment because it prohibits many arrangements under which equipment would be bought.

Although it appears that movement may exist to amend the Stark rules, currently the rules stand "as is" with final regulations due out by the end of 2000.

CHAPTER FIVE

Four Basic Principles
of Compensation

An idea is not responsible for the people who believe in it.
—Don Marquis

Designing an effective physician compensation model requires the buy-in of the physician group. Compensation can be an influential motivator toward desired behavior. However, for the desired results to be achieved, certain basic principles must be in place. A successful plan will motivate physicians to share resources and work together as a team.

PRINCIPLE #1: PHYSICIANS IN THE GROUP MUST TRUST THE FORMULA

Knowledge is power.
—Thomas Hobbes, Leviathan

When change occurs, the natural response is apprehension. This is especially true in the case of compensation formulas. In many cases, physicians already may be apprehensive as to the equality and fairness of the existing formula. Yet however unpopular the existing formula may be, any change may be perceived as threatening.

The key to success and acceptance of change depends on the degree of physician involvement in plan design. If physicians are not involved in the change process, buy-in will most likely not occur. Organizational planning and budgeting is an integral part of compensation design. As part of the plan design, sample formula computations should be prepared based on budgetary expectations so that physicians can see the effects of the new formula on their compensation. If sample computations are not prepared, physicians may reach philosophical decisions that do not provide the desired financial results.

Not only do physicians need to trust the formula, they must trust the individuals assigned the task of administering the formula. The group must have faith in the integrity and competency of those providing the computations. For instance, if physicians perceive favoritism on the part of the individual administering the formula, they are likely to be skeptical as to the equity of the compensation model as a whole.

Additionally, physicians must trust the data used in the compensation computation. If data regarding production, collection, and expenses are continuously flawed and suspect, physicians are unlikely to rely on the results of the model. Reviewing management reports and financial statements with the group is essential in establishing a level of understanding. Physicians must first understand and accept the validity of the existing financial reports before they will feel confident in the use of that data in a compensation formula. Underlying financial data must be consistently reliable in order to garner the trust of the physician group.

Last, physicians must trust each other. If there is inherent mistrust among the physician group regarding patient scheduling and workload, use of resources, and/or quality of care, the formula is likely to fail. The group must develop a cohesiveness and sense of equity regarding core values. Timely, reliable information is key to the establishment of trust within the physician group. Absent hard data, physicians may draw conclusions about members' contributions to the group based on their own perceptions or the perceptions of others. Information is the key to dispel misconceptions based on observation alone.

PRINCIPLE #2: THE FORMULA MUST BE CLEARLY UNDERSTOOD

> *Everything has a moral, if only you can find it.*
> —Lewis Carroll, Alice's Adventures in Wonderland

All too often, compensation models are too complex. In an attempt to achieve equity in allocation, the practice sometimes creates a plan that, for lack of a better description, "splits hairs." The model may result in numerous, complicated spreadsheets and calculations. As the formula becomes more complicated, the purpose of the calculations may become lost in the computations.

Complex formulas lend themselves to error and manipulation. In order for physicians to trust the formula, the calculations must be reliable and must bear some resemblance to the overall financial results of the practice. If the computations are too complex and there is no reconciliation to verifiable financial data (billing reports and financial statements), the results can be manipulated to shift income inappropriately.

For example, consider the situation of a practice in which the compensation of the normally highest-earning physician declines due to the physician not meeting certain formula components. It is often difficult (and politically incorrect) for the administrator/office manager to relay this bad news, especially if it is unexpected. A complex formula may allow for the unnoticed tweaking of certain factors in the calculations in order to waylay this unpleasant task.

Additionally, human nature directs us to distrust those things we do not understand. Complex formulas tend to create distrust among the physician group. If physicians do not understand the formula, they may believe they are being taken advantage of and treated unfairly. The perpetuation of complex models can result in a compensation system that no one understands, even those individuals responsible for calculating the formula.

If the formula is so complex that no one understands the calculations or their purpose, that formula cannot be used as a tool to direct behavior. Physicians must understand the calculations and, most important, must understand how their behavior impacts their compensation. A general rule of thumb is to provide narrative descriptions of the underlying formula to the group with a summary report of compensation amounts, as shown in Exhibit 5.1. Providing pages and pages of spreadsheets with miniscule printing will rarely be understood or used.

EXHIBIT 5.1
Compensation Plan of Best Medical Group

Revenues:
Professional Service Revenues will be allocated 100 percent to the physician providing those services.

Ancillary Service Revenue will be allocated to the ancillary service pool. All costs directly associated with ancillary revenue will reduce the ancillary revenue to create a "net ancillary" service pool. The net ancillary service pool will be distributed equally among all physicians.

Expenses:
One-third of all expenses will be shared equally.

Two-thirds of all expenses will be allocated to each physician based on his/her pro rate share of professional service revenue.

PRINCIPLE #3: THE FORMULA MUST BE EQUITABLE

Compensation models may be equitable; however, as in the book *Animal Farm*, "some may be more equal than others." The basic premise is to establish equality in the computations. Doing so becomes extremely important in multispecialty practices. The allocation of overhead, for instance, must be equitable based on resource utilization. It would be inequitable to allocate overhead on a straight percentage basis in a practice housing both family practice and surgical specialists. The formula may not be "equal", however, equality is established through equitable allocations.

Using our example from the section on the Stark laws, the family practice group has collections from professional services of $500,000 and the surgical group has collections of $1,100,000 for a combined total of $1,600,000. The family practice doctors represent 31.25 percent of total collections; the surgeons represent 68.75 percent. Prior to the merger, the family practice doctors had an overhead rate on professional services of 40 percent ($200,000), while the surgical practice had an overhead rate for professional services of 30 percent ($330,000). Postmerger, the combined practice would have total collections on professional services of $1,600,000 with an overhead rate (total operating expenses associated with professional fees as a percentage of total professional service revenue) of 33 percent. Using collections as the basis for allocating overhead would increase the surgeons' overhead from $330,000 to $364,375 and conversely decrease the family practice group allocation by the same $364,375. For some groups this may not be a problem as there could be other contributing factors that make the merger worthwhile, such as participating in a contract previously shut out of, the creation of a larger pool for sharing even though the overhead is higher, or reducing competition.

PRINCIPLE #4: GROUP INCENTIVES MUST BE PROMOTED

> *If you don't know where you are going*
> *you will probably end up someplace else.*
> —Laurence J. Peter

The fourth principle may very well be the most important in maintaining a successful practice. Physician practices are in a state of transition due to changes in reimbursement, escalating costs, and increasing government regulations. Compensation can be a critical force in supporting change and moving the practice forward and should play a key role in motivating the behaviors needed to effectuate the desired change. There is no doubt that money directs behavior.

A fundamental objective of all compensation plans should be to maintain the financial viability of the group. Without careful, appropriate financial planning and budgeting, practices may set compensation in excess of financial resources, thus setting up the group for failure. Without planning and efficient management, huge losses may occur. Physician compensation models should be designed in a manner that does not jeopardize the financial stability of the group.

In the group practice setting, physician compensation must be considered in the broad context of change initiatives and used to support those initiatives. However, care should be taken not to adopt an innovative approach that does not align with a group's culture or strategic goals. In order to be effective, the compensation model must be in alignment with group goals.

Compensation can be a powerful motivator; however, it cannot influence change if the practice has no strategic objectives. The group must adopt a common philosophy and decide on its desired objectives prior to the design of a compensation plan. The desired organizational behaviors have to be established so that the compensation system can be designed to encourage those behaviors.

For instance, in a fee-for-service environment, productivity still drives revenue. In order for the practice to achieve financial success, physicians must be productive. In this scenario, a compensation formula would want to incorporate factors to motivate physician productivity (i.e., number of visits, hours worked, etc.). All too often, in large group practices, physicians lose sight of the connection between their work effort and practice profitability. Practice consolidators (physician practice management companies [PPMs], hospitals, etc.) have experienced the negative financial effect of physicians who cut back on their hours due to lack of proper incentives to be productive.

On the other hand, groups that are seeking to grow through the addition of physicians, new services, and/or locations may realize a negative effect if compensation is tied strictly to individual productivity. The group must focus on overall practice profitability. In order to facilitate growth, physicians must be encouraged to share their patient load. If the sharing results in significant decreases in the existing physicians' productivity, perhaps the practice should rethink the addition of new providers.

To achieve and maintain long-term success, physician practices must reconsider how they measure value and success. Traditionally, practices have measured success in terms of productivity, cash available, or net income. Although valuable measurements, these primarily relate to short-term results.

In today's competitive environment, the successful group will continue to monitor short-term measures while incorporating other intangibles into the compensation formula. Practices must begin to examine behaviors, organization culture, and operational strategies that will promote long-term success. Factors such as patient satisfaction, outcomes, and quality of care should likewise be considered in the formula.

Defining group strategy is essential to the design of an effective compensation system. The group must decide its direction, goals, and purpose before defining its pay system. The compensation formula must mirror the group strategy and motivate individuals in the appropriate direction for the group to achieve its goals. The plan must be simple enough so that the individual members have a clear understanding of the desired behavior and the manner in which that behavior can impact their compensation.

Well-designed plans establish a true partnership between the group and the individual physician. Core values of trust and respect established between the group and the individual will contribute to the overall organization's performance and achievement of long-term objectives.

In designing a plan, it is important to:

- Model the plan before implementation to make sure it encourages the desired behavior.
- Make certain the data used in the computation is accurate.
- Communicate frequently and regularly—building consensus is essential to success.
- Review the plan frequently in light of organizational or industry changes.
- Not be afraid to change gradually when change is indicated.

CHAPTER SIX

Tax Considerations for Physician Compensation

*The only thing that hurts more than paying an income tax
is not having to pay an income tax.*
—Lord Thomas R. Duwar

The three basic components of a compensation system are:

1. Base salary
2. Incentive pay
3. Benefits

The following chapters discuss all of these compensation components in detail. Base salary and incentive pay (bonus) typically provide a tax deduction for the practice and taxable income for the physician. Fringe benefits, if properly structured, may provide a tax deduction for the practice while providing the physician with a tax-free benefit.

Medical group practices may choose from three main types of business entities for tax purposes:

1. General Partnership
2. Limited Liability Company
3. Professional corporation—"C" corp. or "S" corp.

GENERAL PARTNERSHIPS

A "partnership" includes a syndicate, group, pool, joint venture, or other unincorporated organization through which the business of the practice is conducted. By definition, a partnership must have at least two members. For tax purposes, the partnership is a pass-through entity whereby income less expenses are "passed through" to the owners based on ownership or some other predetermined means of profit sharing. Physicians are taxed individually on their respective share of the partnership's income.

Until the advent of the professional corporation in 1970 (Rev. Rul. 70–101, 1970–1 CB 278), the partnership structure was the only organizational option available for group practices. The general partnership provides tax flexibility for admitting physicians as owners as well as retiring physician members. Additionally, unreasonable compensation, which may be an issue with owner-employees in professional corporations, is a nonissue with a partnership structure.

The general partnership, however, provides no protection from a legal liability standpoint. A physician is personally liable for his or her own acts of malpractice regardless of the practice entity (professional corporation or limited liability company). However, in a general partnership, the partners are jointly and severally liable individually for the acts of each member.

According to the Medical Group Managers Association *Cost Survey: 1999 Report Based on 1998 Data*, only 4.32 percent of the responding practices operate as general partnerships. The percentage has decreased from the 1993 report, which indicated that 8.07 percent of the respondents were organized as a partnership. The reduction is due, in part, to the advent of the limited liability company.

LIMITED LIABILITY COMPANIES

Limited liability companies (LLCs) are a creation of state law. LLCs are owned (in some cases managed) by members who are not personally liable for the LLC's debts or obligations. The LLC may be classified as a partnership for federal tax purposes, thus offering the flexibility of the "pass-through" entity combined with limited liability previously afforded only to corporations. Additionally, in some states, a limited liability company may be organized with one member.

According to the MGMA's 1999 Report, 5.67 percent of the respondents utilized the LLC structure. As with the general partnerships, members report LLC net income on their individual income tax returns based on their respective profit-sharing percentage. Because of the "pass-through" nature of profit distribution, unreasonable compensation is not an issue with LLCs.

PROFESSIONAL CORPORATIONS

According to the MGMA's 1999 Report, the majority of the respondents, 64.55 percent, had elected professional corporation as their legal organizational form. The survey does not differentiate between Sub S corporations and Regular C corporations. Sub S corporations pass income to physicians in the form of compensation but also pass net income to shareholders and, in general, do not pay federal tax at the corporate level. Regular C corporations that retain income at the corporate level would pay a corporate-level tax and physician employees would pay tax on their W-2 compensation.

From a tax standpoint, a professional corporation or association may pay a reasonable salary for personal services rendered (Sec. 162 [a]). However, the Internal Revenue Service may deny deductions to the corporation for payments that exceed a reasonable amount.

The Revenue Reconciliation Act of 1993 imposed a special limitation for the deduction of executive compensation for publicly traded corporations that are listed on a national securities exchange with more than $5 million in assets and 500 or more shareholders. (Sec. 162 [m]). These entities may not deduct more than $1 million annually for the compensation of a chief executive officer and the four highest paid officers other than the chief executive officer. Although this section of the tax law will not apply to most group practices (except those owned by large hospital chains and/or publicly traded practice management companies), the implications may be carried forward to physician practices.

For federal tax purposes, corporations other than personal service corporations and foreign corporations have a graduated tax scale of 15 to 35 percent based on their net income. Personal service corporations, which include incorporated medical practices incorporated under chapter C of the Internal Revenue Code, are currently taxed at a federal flat rate of 35 percent. This unfavorable rate is imposed based on the premise that the personal service corporation's revenue comes from the performance of personal services that are substantially performed by the employee-owners.

The definition of a personal service corporation should provide protection from unreasonable compensation claims. By definition, the income comes from the personal service of the owner-employee, and the corporation may deduct a reasonable allowance for salaries paid for personal services rendered. However, the IRS has raised issues of unreasonable compensation in medical practice audits.

One such case is *Richlands Medical Association v. Commissioner* (Docket No. 16595-86, TC Memo. 1990-660, 60 TCM 1572, Filed December 31, 1990). In 1962, Richlands Medical Association (the petitioner) was organized pursuant to the Professional Association Act of Virginia, section 54-873 et seq., Code of Virginia (the Virginia act), for purposes including the practice of medicine and the operation of a general hospital. In accordance with the Virginia act, articles of association were adopted for the petitioner.

On October 26, 1981, Richlands Medical Association's articles of association were amended. The amended articles of association remained in effect throughout the years in issue, in addition to the association's bylaws.

The owners, or "members," of a professional association organized under the Virginia act are referred to as its "associates," and each associate is entitled to a "certificate of ownership" evidencing the proportional part of the association he or she owns. The Virginia act also provides that all associates of a professional association must be employees of the association and must be licensed to practice the profession for which the association is organized.

Richlands Medical Association listed four associates (Drs. McVey, Strader, Moore, and Khuri). Dr. Strader died during the taxable year ended October 31, 1982, and this certificate of ownership was returned to Richlands Medical Association. Drs. McVey, Moore, and Khuri were the sole members during the tax years in issue and also constituted the board of directors.

The bylaws for Richlands Medical Association provided that the board of directors could hold their meetings at such times and places as it might designate, but was required to hold at least one meeting per quarter. During the taxable years in issue, the board held at least 26 meetings, and the minutes of which were recorded. At those meetings, a variety of matters relating to the operation of the hospital were discussed and voted upon, including: hiring decisions with respect to nonowner physicians, collections, pay raises and other personnel matters, purchases and leases of property, pension matters litigation, and retention of accountants. The meetings sometimes were called on very short notice, depending on the urgency of the matters requiring attention.

The bylaws provided for the employment of a hospital administrator who was to act as the board's representative in the management of the hospital. The hospital administrator, however, was required to obtain approval from the board for all expenditures necessary to the everyday operation of the hospital in excess of $1,000.

During the years in issue, the members were compensated as follows:

	Year Ended 10/31/82	Year Ended 10/31/83
McVey	$977,778	$873,298
Khuri	702,524	672,871
Moore	566,522	523,831

The IRS allowed in its notice of deficiency a compensation deduction with respect to each member equal to 100 percent of the collections recorded by the physician as attributable to medical services performed directly for patients by such physician. Additionally, the association was permitted to deduct reasonable compensation for the associates' performance of duties as heads of various hospital departments and as officers of the association. A portion of the association's claimed deductions for reasonable compensation was denied, in part due to the pattern of compensating associates in a manner that would never result in funds available for the payment of dividends.

Tax deficiencies assessed were as follows:

10/31/82	$637,376
10/31/83	602,207

The IRS also ruled that a portion of the medical association's underpayment was due to negligence. The association operated a hospital, and the hospital's bylaws provided for a year-end distribution of net profits based on ownership. It was unreasonable to claim a deduction for reasonable compensation in a manner that eliminated the association's net profit available to distribute as dividends.

Negligence penalties were assessed as follows:

10/31/82	$31,869
10/31/83	$30,111

The following chart illustrates the amount of collections allowed along with gross charges for the medical services of each physician:

	10/31/82 Billings	Collections	10/31/83 Billings	Collections
McVey	$622,260	$397,556	$592,470	$324,759
Khuri	363,641	241,014	426,434	231,435
Moore	310,204	191,714	302,641	162,467

A comparison of the compensation paid to each associate with billings and collections indicates that each associate was paid, during the years at issue, not only substantially more than the collections recorded for his personal services but also substantially more than the billings for his services. For example, Dr. McVey's pay for the year ended 10/31/82 was approximately 157 percent of his billings and 246 percent of his collections. Dr. Khuri's pay for such year was approximately 193 percent of billings and 291 percent of collections.

Dr. McVey's specialty was family medicine. On a daily basis, Monday through Friday, he saw an average of 60 outpatients. On Saturdays he saw an average of 30 to 40 outpatients. Additionally, he saw approximately 40 inpatients on a daily basis.

Dr. Khuri practiced general and thoracic surgery and also served as president of Richlands Medical Association. He worked at the hospital about 55 to 60 hours per week in addition to hours "on call." He saw an average of approximately 25 outpatients and 7 to 8 inpatients per day at the hospital.

There were no employment contracts fixing the remuneration of the physicians. The bylaws provided that: "The Board of Directors at the end of the fiscal year shall divide the net profits in the following manner: 25 percent of the profits shall be divided equally among the associates, and the remaining 75 percent shall be divided according to each associate's productivity factor, the factor being his total net collections and the denominator being the total net collections of all associates."

Among Drs. McVey, Khuri, and Moore, relative compensation during the years at issue was roughly proportional to relative collections, as illustrated in the following chart:

10/31/82	Individual Collections as a % of Total Collections	Individual Compensation as a % of Total Compensation
McVey	48%	44%
Khuri	29%	31%
Moore	23%	25%
10/31/83		
McVey	45%	42%
Khuri	32%	33%
Moore	23%	25%

(Collections and compensation of Dr. Strader, who died during the year ended 10/31/82, have been ignored for purposes of these computations.)

During the years at issue, Richlands Medical Associates employed other physicians, in addition to its associates, to work in the hospital. There were eight such nonowner physicians during the year ended 10/31/82 and 10 such physicians during the year ended 10/31/83. The nonowner physicians employed at the hospital entered into written employment contracts with Richlands Medical. These contracts indicated that the physicians generally were paid on the basis of a fixed salary or a percentage of annual collections, whichever was greater, with such percentages ranging from 85 to 110 percent of collections. Neither the associates nor the nonowner physicians paid rent for the use of the hospital facilities and equipment or paid the other expenses (such as nurses' salaries) associated with private practice.

When a patient was treated at the hospital, the hospital issued a single bill that included charges for the physician's professional services and for other hospital services and items. Included within the hospital component of the bill were charges for "ancillary services" such as anesthesia, operating room, recovery room, drugs, Xrays, and the like. In the event that a bill was not paid in full and the payor failed to designate whether the payment was to be applied to the physician or the hospital component, the practice was to treat the payment as attributable to the hospital component up to the amount of such hospital charges. Nondesignated partial payments sometimes occurred in the case of payments made directly by patients and also occurred in the case of payments by certain private insurance companies. With respect to payments received from Blue Cross/Blue Shield, all amounts from Blue Shield were allocated to physician services, and all amounts from Blue Cross and other government insurance programs were designated as attributable to either physician or hospital services.

Richlands Medical Associates' practice of allocating nondesignated partial payments to hospital charges had the effect of reducing the "collections" recorded for its physicians. As noted above, nonowner physicians generally were compensated based on a fixed salary or percentage of such collections, whichever was greater. For the taxable year ended 10/31/82, the association's highest paid nonowner physician received a salary of $146,574. For the taxable year ended 10/31/83, the salary was $214,012.

The hospital designated a full-time administrator in February 1982. The administrator was paid $86,863 for the taxable year ended 10/31/82 and $95,536 for the taxable year ended 10/31/83. The bylaws required the hospital administrator to attend all meetings of the board of directors for the association and outlined his or her duties, which included:

1. Supervision of all business affairs of the hospital such as records of financial transaction, collection of accounts, and purchase and issuance of supplies and drugs
2. Submission of monthly reports to the board of directors showing the professional service and financial activities of the hospital
3. Annual submission to the board of directors of a plan of organization of personnel and others concerned with hospital operation
4. Serving as a liaison between the association's board of directors and the hospital's medical staff

5. Enforcing all rules and regulations for the conduct of the hospital made by and under the authority of the board of directors

6. Responsibility for overseeing the physical condition and repair of the hospital properties

The compensation received by the members of the association during the years at issue substantially exceeded amounts received in prior years. While the association's gross income also increased over the same period, the increases in gross income were relatively small in comparison with the increases in compensation. The following chart illustrates the increases in the association's gross income during a six-year period ending with the years at issue.

Year Ended	Gross Income
10/31/78	$4,642,842
10/31/79	5,323,688
10/31/80	6,378,191
10/31/81	7,378,715
10/31/82	9,951,916
10/31/83	10,308,289

Exhibit 6.1 illustrates the increases in compensation and collections of Drs. McVey, Khuri, and Moore during the same six-year period. As indicated, the increases in compensation that occurred starting with the years at issue were also high in relation in increases in collections.

Thus, between the years ended 10/31/78 and 10/31/81, Dr. McVey's compensation averaged approximately 121 percent of his collections. For the years at issue, however, his compensation averaged approximately 256 percent of his collections. Similarly, Dr. Moore's compensation for the years

EXHIBIT 6.1
Collections and Compensation During Six-Year Period

Taxable Year	Dr. McVey		Dr. Khuri		Dr. Moore	
	Collections	Compensation	Collections	Compensation	Collections	Compensation
10/31/78	$249,254	$378,000	$101,600	$95,000	$76,311	$127,042
10/31/79	281,084	273,408	159,223	192,383	95,318	124,274
10/31/80	313,019	345,870	240,742	285,828	150,218	198,530
10/31/81	308,121	397,714	181,838	261,450	150,822	228,244
10/31/82	397,556	977,778	241,014	702,524	191,714	566,552
10/31/83	324,759	873,298	231,436	672,871	162,468	523,831

ended 10/31/78 through 10/31/81 averaged approximately 143 percent of his collections while his compensation for the years at issue averaged approximately 308 percent of collections.

During the years at issue, the Virginia act conveyed on the board of directors of a professional association the right to fix the amount and method of compensation of association employees as well as the right to "set up reserves or distribute excess earnings to each of the associates in proportion to his ownership in the association." Richlands Medical Association's bylaws provided for the distribution to its associates of all of the association's "net profits" each year. The association treated all payments to its associates as compensation and did not treat any of such payments as dividends.

Richlands Medical Association amended its petition to claim partnership status. During the years at issue, all income and expenses were reported as a corporation (form 1120). The petition was denied based on the tax court's opinion that the entity possessed the characteristics of continuity of life and centralized management.

A summary of the facts indicates that:

- Richlands Medical Association compensated its owner-physicians in excess of nonowner physicians and physicians in similar specialties.
- The owner-physicians did not have employment agreements.
- The association combined revenues from personal services (medical practice) with significant revenue from other sources (hospital).
- Compensation to owner-physicians was in excess of their collections from their direct medical services.

The Richlands Medical Association decision serves as a warning to medical groups that do not follow "business protocol." Corporate status requires that certain criteria be met, such as employment agreements and minutes of meetings. It is obvious that the compensation plan of the Richlands group was not well documented as to the valuing of the physicians' personal services.

Furthermore, the group combined personal service income (the medical group practice) and nonpersonal service income (the hospital). Care should be taken in developing compensation plans for groups with significant income not derived from physicians' personal services. An example might be an orthopedic practice that maintains a large physical therapy clinic. In this case, the Stark rules would prohibit placing the physical therapy clinic in a separate entity. However, appropriate assignment of direct and indirect expenses to the clinic may assist in reducing potential unreasonable compensation considerations.

The reasonable test is a factual one. As such, it is not measured by specific percentage thresholds or dollar amounts. The regulations offer the following guidelines:

- The relationship between the salaries and ownership is considered. Salaries to owners must be reasonable when compared to salaries paid to nonowners for similar services. In other words, if a practice employs both owner and nonowner physicians, the differential in compensation should be documented based on services provided, experience, qualifications, and the like.
- The compensation for comparable services in the industry is considered. The IRS has used the Medical Group Management Association surveys to define the industry standard. In situations where practices compensate physicians substantially in excess of the MGMA median, the excess should be documented based on the effort (personal service) of the physicians. If the excess is the result of earnings from ancillary services (i.e., physical therapy services), the practice must be ready to defend its payment of additional compensation to the physician-owners.
- Whether the compensation was a result of arm's length bargaining is considered as a factor. This evidence can include written employment contracts.

As in the Richlands case, the IRS and the courts use the following 12 factors to determine whether the amount of compensation is reasonable (IRC Sec. 162):

1. Employee's qualifications, including any special training and experience
2. Nature, extent, and scope of the employee's work
3. Size and complexity of the business
4. Employee's knowledge of the business
5. Employee's contribution to profit making
6. Prevailing rates of compensation for other comparable positions
7. Relationship of the shareholder's compensation to stockholdings
8. Time devoted by the employee to the business
9. Economic conditions in general and locally
10. Time of year when compensation is determined

11. Whether alleged compensation is in reality, in whole or in part, payment for a business or assets acquired
12. Character and amount of responsibility of the employee

The Hospital Audit Guidelines at Section 331 (1) list the following 10 factors as relevant in determining the reasonableness of compensation:

1. Duties performed and amount of responsibility
2. Time devoted to duties
3. Special knowledge and experience
4. Individual ability
5. Previous training
6. Compensation paid in prior years
7. Working conditions
8. Prevailing general economic conditions (including wage levels for work of similar scope and nature, price levels, and inflation)
9. Living conditions in the particular locality
10. Comparability to similar positions in similar entities

The most common challenge to compensation paid to a stockholder-employee is that all or a portion of it should be characterized as a dividend. Salary amounts that are deemed to be unreasonable typically are reclassified as dividends. Failure to pay dividends is not conclusive evidence that compensation is a disguised dividend, but it may be a significant factor. A legitimate business reason for not paying dividends, such as the need to conserve capital for expansion, can rebut the presumption. Dividends are not deductible for the personal service corporation (taxed at 35 percent) and are taxable as ordinary income to the shareholder (maximum rate 39.6 percent).

The IRS has used a number of factors and arguments to support reclassification of salaries as dividend payments. Some of these factors include:

- A compensation system that is proportionate with ownership interests (i.e., a bonus of profits to the physician-owners based on the percentage of ownership interests). Close correspondence between compensation and stockholdings is especially likely to invite a challenge when the compensation is paid in the form of year-end bonuses determined after corporate profits for the year are known.
- The complete absence of formal dividend distributions by an expanding business.

- Bonus payments that are made only to officer-shareholders and to no other employees.

- An ill-defined bonus system that appears to be a function of corporate earnings rather than shareholder services. Retroactive determinations of compensation are not distributions of profits per se, but they are given close scrutiny because they may indicate an intention to distribute a disguised dividend.

- Salaries that are not comparable to similar services in the industry. Additionally, compensation paid to a shareholder-employee that is clearly in excess of the compensation of similar employees who are not shareholders is apt to be recharacterized as a dividend if the difference cannot be explained by differences in duties or responsibilities. The excess amount is particularly likely to be disallowed if it coincides with what would have been the shareholder-employee's allocable share of corporate net earnings available for distribution.

- Incentive payments that do not have a true compensatory purpose. Incentive compensation based on a gross margin formula may be considered a disguised dividend. Generally more leeway is allowed in the case of personal service corporations, when the success of the business is almost entirely dependent on the efforts of the officers.

Pass-through entities such as subchapter S corporations, partnerships, and limited liability companies can use their ability to pass income to physician-owners via distributions to avoid the unreasonable compensation issue. In pass-through entities, physicians are taxed on their compensation (or guaranteed payment in the case of a partnership or limited liability company) and their respective share of the practice profits. The entities themselves (with the exception of built-in gains tax with S corporations) pay no tax.

Careful consideration must be given to choosing the form of practice entity for tax purposes. S corporations, for instance, only can make dividend distributions proportionate to stock ownership. If the dividend distributions were to constitute the incentive portion of the physician compensation model, the methodology would be limited based on ownership of stock regardless of the physician's efforts. Additionally, tax-free benefits are not available (i.e., disability insurance) or are reduced (health insurance) in this type of entity.

The potential for unreasonable compensation further substantiates the benefits of a documented compensation model that rewards physicians based on their services to the group. Many of the points considered by the IRS in determining reasonable compensation (i.e., qualifications, complexity of the job, productivity of the individual) are sound components for a physician compensation model.

Incorporated medical practices likewise must take care in the use of the corporate bank account to ensure that corporate funds are not misused for personal purposes. When the physician-owner withdraws personal funds from the corporate bank account (with the exception of salary), many times these withdrawals are treated by the corporation as loans to the stockholder (physician receiving the benefit).

If the corporation loans funds to a stockholder, the transaction must be at arm's length. The stockholder must provide the corporation with a signed note bearing a reasonable (market) interest rate. The note should be repaid according to the schedule provided in the note instrument.

Absent the above, the IRS may reclassify the stockholder loan as a disguised dividend. Additionally, Section 7872 of the Internal Revenue Code addresses the implications of below-market loans. The general effect of Section 7872 is that it recharacterizes a below-market loan as an arm's-length transaction in which the lender makes a loan to the borrower in exchange for a note requiring the payment of interest at a statutory rate. As a result, the parties are treated as if the lender made a transfer of funds to the borrower and the borrower used these funds to pay interest to the lender. The transfer to the borrower is treated as a gift, a dividend, a contribution of capital, a payment of compensation, or another payment, depending on the substance of the transaction. The imputed interest payment is in the professional corporation's income and would be subject to the 35 percent federal tax.

CHAPTER SEVEN

Employment Agreements

It is undesirable to believe a proposition
when there is no ground whatsoever for supposing it true.
—Bertrand Russell

A compensation plan should be detailed in an employment agreement that is a legal contract between the practice and the physician. The employment agreement should address all the pertinent issues of the compensation plan. For tax purposes, the employment agreement is an integral component to establish the basis for reasonable compensation in an incorporated practice. From a legal standpoint, the employment agreement memorializes the agreement between the physician and the practice and can prevent misunderstandings concerning aspects of the compensation plan.

A written employment agreement may protect the physician in the following ways:

- A written agreement clarifies expectations. A written agreement will assist in clarifying the roles and responsibilities of both the physician and the practice. For instance, such an agreement not only defines the amount and methodology of compensation but also specifies the duties required to earn that compensation.

- A written agreement provides information on incentive opportunities. The agreement should clearly state the goals and behaviors that will result in additional compensation for the physician. Additionally, for the nonowner employee, options for buy-in also may be specified.

- A written agreement makes negotiations easier. Communication may become distorted in oral agreements. A written agreement memorializes oral discussions and makes negotiation on specific points more effective. The drafting of the documents and related discussions provide invaluable insight for the new physician regarding the practice's organization and culture. For example, is the practice reluctant to provide financial information? This may be a sign of inefficient management and/or poor financial reporting. Keep in mind that the agreement is not effective until it is signed.

Ninety percent of the negotiation effort should be dedicated to prenegotiation planning. The planning phase should clarify priorities, objectives, and contingencies. The process begins with a thorough review of any existing contracts. This review typically includes an assessment of the following needs:

- Clarification or modification based on events or changes that have occurred
- Removal of obsolete provisions that no longer apply in the current healthcare environment
- Updating relevant data for productivity, quality, compensation, and benefits
- Revisiting the role boundaries and expectations of both parties to the agreement
- Incorporating any new requirements resulting from organization, regulatory, or marketplace changes

The negotiating process should be a collaborative problem-solving endeavor. Ideally, both sides should emerge with a renewed sense of respect.

A written agreement may outline the methodology for protecting current agreements in the event of potential mergers and/or acquisitions. The agreements may provide some protection of assets, such as deferred compensation and/or other accrued benefits, in the event that the practice ultimately merges or is acquired.

The employment agreement should be reviewed on an annual basis. Many times practices change their compensation methodology without changing their employment agreements. In those cases, a disagreement about computations may lead to expensive litigation. Any revisions to allocation of Stark revenues (designated health services) should be made prospectively and should not be revised other than on an annual basis.

Legal assistance is recommended to properly design employment agreements. Each attorney may have a unique style for the wording of the agreement; however, every agreement should include the following six categories:

1. Introduction. The introduction section of the employment agreement typically sets forth the legal names of the parties to the agreement, the address of the parties, and the intent of the agreement.

2. Premise. The agreement usually contains a section covering the relationship between the parties (i.e., the employer is a multispecialty group practice and the employee is a licensed family practice physician) and the premise of the contract (i.e., the practice desires to employ the physician and the physician desires to be employed to provide medical care to the practice's patients).

3. Term. The term of the agreement, as well as options available to extend the agreement, should be specified. Most physician contracts have terms from one to five years. The contract, however, may be a fixed-term contract in which no renewal terms are included and the issue is left to renegotiation as the contract nears its end. An evergreen contract is one in which there is always a remaining term equal to the original term. That is, as each day passes, the term of the contract automatically is extended by a day. These are usually shorter-term contracts and rarely have terms greater than three years. Modified evergreen contracts are contracts in which the term is extended automatically at its conclusion for successive periods (usually one year) unless the practice notifies the physician of its intention not to renew. Such notice generally is required at least six months before the contract would otherwise expire.

4. Compensation and benefits. The contract either may include the compensation plan or may reference the plan as an exhibit to the employment agreement. In either case, the compensation plan should be clearly defined in the body of the employment agreement or by exhibit. Base salary, if provided, should be established. If the plan provides for incentive compensation, the methodology for determining the incentive amount should be defined. Careful consideration should be given to the Stark rules and income tax regulations in determining the incentive formula.

   Fringe benefits typically are covered in general terms in the employment contract. The employment contract may simply provide that the physician is to be covered by all employee benefit plans provided by the practice in which he or she is eligible to participate. Additionally, the employment agreement may state that the physician recognizes that the benefits and plans will change from time to time and that his or her benefits will change accordingly. A nonspecific reference to benefits will provide the group practice with the flexibility to change and/or amend plans without the necessity of generating new employment agreements each time a change or amendment takes place.

Vacations, holidays, professional meetings, and other time-off benefits should be addressed. For example, does the practice provide time off from regular duties to teach, conduct research, or serve on professional organization committees and boards? Is there a provision for leaves of absence for family or maternity leave?

The agreement may provide for "x" number of working days out of the office to cover all time off (vacation, holidays, sick, continuing medical education, etc.). The agreement may likewise set dollar limits (i.e., $5,000 annually) that the practice will provide for continuing education costs and travel.

5. Termination provisions. The agreement should address the events that would cause the termination of employment. Death, retirement, and disability should be addressed as well as termination due to conduct. If the practice provides for salary continuation in the event of death or disability, the employment contract should provide the methodology for computing the continuation amount.

   Certain events, such as the loss of a medical license, conviction of a felony or some misdemeanor, automatically will cause termination. Additionally, the agreement may provide for automatic termination if the practice becomes bankrupt or dissolves.

   The agreement also may provide for termination "without cause." The without-cause provision typically will require a certain written notice period (i.e., 120 days).

6. Duties and responsibilities. The employment agreement should specify the required duties and responsibilities for employment. For example, the agreement should state that the physician actively practices medicine on behalf of the practice. Additionally, the agreement may indicate that the physician agrees to comply with policies, procedures, and operational guidelines regarding the acceptance and treatment of patients of the practice. The physician should be required to adhere to all professional ethics and customs, and agree to avoid all acts, habits, and usages that might injure in any way, directly or indirectly, the professional reputation of the practice. He or she should likewise agree to follow all federal, state, and municipal ordinances and laws relating to or regulating the practice of medicine. The agreement may provide for the disciplinary steps that will be taken by the practice in the event of noncompliance to conduct standards.

More and more, group practices are requesting their physicians to participate in certain management activities. Likewise, physicians are seeking greater clarity on specific responsibilities, authorities, and participation in the decision-making process. A thoughtfully drafted position description can go a long way toward clarifying these mutual expectations.

As an appendix to the agreement, the following administrative duties may likewise be addressed:

- Medical administration duties (policy, procedures, budgets, etc.)
- Physician relations (communications, recruiting, problem resolution)
- Clinical administration (quality, utilization, outcomes)
- Education and staff development (educational development for physicians and nonphysicians)
- Business development (program growth, integration, promotion)

7. Administrative guidelines. The employment agreement may provide certain administrative guidelines. For example, the agreement may provide that the practice will establish all professional fees for services rendered by the physician. Likewise, the agreement may specify that all collections and billings arising pursuant to the rendering of medical services by the physician are owned and controlled by the practice and are thus assigned to the practice. Custodial responsibilities of the physician may be included in the agreement, including the physician's responsibility to maintain full and accurate accounts and records of all professional work performed in a timely fashion in accordance with guidelines established by the practice. An agreement by the practice to provide the office space, equipment, and other necessary items for the physician to practice medicine can be included in this section. Additionally, provisions for the maintenance of malpractice coverage may be addressed.

8. Restrictive covenant (noncompete agreements). The parties to the employment agreement may stipulate that, in the event of termination, the physician will agree not to compete with the practice. The agreement typically will specify a reasonable period of time that the agreement not to compete will be in effect after termination. The geographic area covered by the noncompete covenant will be identified. Additionally, the agreement may provide that the departing physician will not solicit or employ existing practice staff. The agreement may provide for remedies in the event of a breach of this section.

In general, the more reasonable noncompete agreements are, the more likely they are to be enforced by the courts. Courts generally consider three issues when determining if a noncompete covenant is reasonable:

1. The length of the postemployment, noncompete period
2. The geographical area in which the physician is prohibited from competing
3. Whether the restrictions are reasonably necessary to protect the legitimate business interests of the practice

Additionally, the employment agreement may provide a stipulation that requires the physician not to disclose confidential information during the term of the agreement. Confidential information may be defined as all materials, information, and ideas of the practice including, without limitation: patient names, lists, records, and information; operation methods and information; accounting and financial and fee information; marketing and pricing information and materials; internal publications and memoranda; and other matters considered confidential by the practice.

Enforcement of restrictive covenants will vary from state to state. Most contracts, however, include noncompete language that is designed to protect the business interests of the practice. The employer maintains that the covenant is necessary due to the unique nature of medicine and the reliance of the practice upon the services of the physician. When the physician leaves the practice and stays in the same geographic area, his or her patients typically follow. This situation may expose the practice to financial loss. In order to be enforceable, the terms of the noncompete covenant must be reasonable.

Adequacy of consideration is one factor that courts consider when deciding whether a covenant not to compete is enforceable. Future employment may well constitute sufficient consideration for a covenant not to compete in an original contract for a new employee.

The more difficult question is whether continued employment of an existing employee is sufficient consideration for a covenant not to compete executed after employment has begun. Courts have provided some assistance in determining whether continued employment will provide sufficient consideration to support a covenant not to compete that is signed during the course of employment. Employment for only a short period of time, for instance, may be insufficient consideration under some circumstances.

Another factor to consider is the circumstances under which the employee left. If an existing employee chooses to leave voluntarily after signing a restrictive covenant, then more than likely the consideration of future employment will be determined to be adequate. If, however, the employee is arbitrarily discharged, the court may be less likely to support continued employment as adequate consideration.

The circumstances under which the agreement was signed also appear to bear on the adequacy of consideration. If the employee can prove that the contract was signed under duress, it may not be enforceable.

For any noncompete agreement to be enforceable, the competition that is sought to be restrained must be more than ordinary competition. Only competition that is gained unfairly can be prohibited in a noncompete agreement. Protectable business interest that may justify imposition of a noncompete covenant include:

- Retention of existing customers (patients)
- Protection of trade secrets
- Employer's investment in training the employee

The most applicable of these factors in the medical practice is the first, retention of existing patients. An employer is entitled to protection through noncompetition agreements if it can demonstrate that a special relationship developed between the employee and the customer while the employee represented the employer. The courts describe this relationship as one "where the employee closely associates or has repeated contact with the employer's customers so that the customer tends to associate the employer's business with the employee." This is certainly the scenario in the case of a physician-patient relationship. Although patients maintain a relationship with the medical group, their primary relationship is with the physician who cares for them. If a physician leaves a medical group and enters into competition with it, the practice may be able to enforce a noncompete agreement based on the patient-physician relationship.

Because noncompete agreements are restraints on trade, they are strictly construed under state law. Any ambiguity in a covenant not to compete generally is construed against the drafter (typically the employer) in favor of competition and in favor of the employee. In the case of *Homebound Medical Care v. Hospital Staffing Services* (1998 Tenn. App. LEXIS 93, (February 6, 1995), the employee entered into an employment agreement with a one-year, nonrenewable term of employment and with a covenant not to compete lasting "for a period of three (3) years from the date of his separation from such employment." After the one-year term expired, the employee continued to remain employed for three more years before resigning and joining a competitor nine months later. The Court of Appeals held that the noncompete period had already expired, finding the term "separation" from employment to be ambiguous and construing it to mean the date of expiration of the term of the employment agreement. In support, the court noted another provision in the employment agreement stating that the termination of the employment agreement shall not invalidate the covenant not to compete, "except to the extent it may establish a date of separation."

Ordinarily, the measure of damages for violation of a noncompete covenant is the profits lost as a result of the breach. More specifically, the employer's lost net profits are ordinarily the proper measure of recovery. Therefore, proof of the employer's net profits before and after the employee's violation of the noncompete agreement generally is required. Restrictive covenant agreements likewise can set forth liquidated damages to be awarded in the case of a breach.

Injunctive relief can be sought as a remedy for breach. In granting injunctive relief, state courts may adopt the federal requirements that require a plaintiff to demonstrate one or more of four situations:

1. A substantial likelihood of success on the merits
2. Irreparable and immediate harm
3. The relative harm that will result to each party as a result of the disposition of the application for injunction
4. That the public interest is served by issuance of an injunction

An employment agreement assists in defining the relationship and responsibilities between the physician and the practice as well as the methodology for compensation. The agreement should cover all key points of the relationship, and legal counsel should be obtained to draft the final documents.

CHAPTER EIGHT

Base Salary

There is no more delicate matter to take in hand, nor more dangerous to conduct, nor more doubtful to success, than to step up as a leader in the introduction of changes. For he who innovates will have for his enemies all those who are well off under the existing order of things, and only lukewarm supporters in those who might be better off under the new
—Niccolo Machiavelli

Base salary comprises the guaranteed portion of the physician's compensation package providing the physician with compensation for the core aspects of his or her duties. Base salary is a regular, fixed component of physician compensation. It reflects the competitive value of the physician's specialty, skills, and experience. Base salary establishes financial security, a known or given amount on at least a monthly basis. The amount of base compensation must be sufficient to meet the physician's minimum financial security needs.

In the case of employee (nonowner) physicians, base salary may constitute their entire compensation package. This is especially true for new physicians (new recruits) joining an existing group practice.

When new physicians are added to a group practice, the goal should be to incorporate them into the practice by effectively guiding them toward being effective members of the group. Although productivity is an important factor in physician behavior, it should not be considered in a vacuum. Other factors such as quality care, resource conservation, patient satisfaction, and group mentality should be developed and encouraged with new associates.

In order to effectively recruit the best and the brightest, the base salary offered must be competitive. However, keep in mind that the beginning salary sets the stage for future expectations. Therefore, the initial base compensation offered to new recruits must be realistic within the parameters of the group and the group's financial budget. As an unknown Chinese philosopher stated, "Only offer to another what you can deliver."

Compensation for new physicians may include a semiannual or annual bonus based on an evaluation of overall performance. Factors used in the evaluation may include practice growth and individual effort. This type of evaluation requires a level of trust on the part of new physicians and may lay the groundwork for a stronger relationship with the group in the future. Recruits who are not able to be productive without a large incentive may not be a good fit for a medical group practice.

Institutions and integrated healthcare delivery systems may utilize a base salary method whereby the base salary is predetermined for a given period and negotiated based on performance. This system occurs rarely in the group practice setting as it does not include any incentive and requires strong management.

In certain formulas (eat what you kill), the base salary may constitute an advance against actual results. In other formula calculations, incentive pay may be calculated without regard to base salary. An example of both methods will be examined further in this book.

One danger in setting base salaries lies in the encouragement of complacency among the physician group. Physician practice management companies (PPMs) and hospitals have experienced the detrimental effects of setting physician base compensation too high. Physicians must not operate under a sense of entitlement but must be challenged to perform. There must be some degree of shared risk between the group and the individual physician.

Base salary cannot be used as an effective means to direct behavior and, therefore, should not exceed 80 percent of projected compensation. The incentive pool should be at least 20 percent in order to be a meaningful motivator. The higher the salary base, the more this method resembles equal compensation methodology.

In order to establish base salary at 80 percent of projected compensation, the practice must have some idea of what projected compensation should be. One method of establishing the base salary is to utilize 80 percent of the national average by specialty. Another method would be to use historical data of the practice. The ideal method is to develop a budget for the upcoming year. Therefore, the practice must establish a realistic budget to set base salaries appropriately. Without an operational budget, base compensation may be set at a level that would endanger the financial stability of the group.

PREPARING THE BUDGET

An operating budget for the practice is an essential tool in physician compensation planning. Furthermore, a well-constructed practice budget is a management tool, a method to institute plans and provide internal controls, a way to gather vital information about the practice, and a strategy to translate goals into defined benchmarks.

The budget is also more than a set of numbers. It is a numerical statement of how the medical practice operates, what it accomplishes, and where it is headed. Establishment of a budget is a dynamic process. The budgeting process should be considered successful if it allows a practice to:

- Determine and set its priorities
- Allocate its resources
- Monitor its revenues
- Control its costs
- Achieve its established priorities

Any budget contains certain common elements, whether it is a budget for a construction company or a budget for a medical practice. Of course, some budget elements are unique to particular businesses. That is especially true of the complicated financial variables encountered in a medical practice. The basic elements of any budget consist of:

- Revenue budget (projected income from all sources)
- Expense budget (projected outlay of money for both variable and fixed expenses)
- Changes in assets (capital acquisitions or sales)
- Changes in debt (acquisitions, retirement of financial obligations)
- Compensation (base salary, bonuses, benefits)

Other budget considerations include strategic planning decisions regarding overall goals. These decisions may include:

- Expansion to new locations
- Personnel dynamics (new staff, retirement of staff, shift to part-time status)
- Addition of new modalities (laboratory, radiology)

REVENUES

The key projection in any operating budget is operating revenues. To determine the practice income, fee-for-service (FFS) charge projections must be calculated. These projections are based on past activities. The underlying assumption is that the best indicator of a physician's activity level for next year is what he or she is doing today.

Management should determine, based on established goals and market factors, adjustments to historical data that will affect the revenue budget. Will there be a fee increase, and if so, what impact will those increases have on revenues? How many patients does the practice anticipate seeing daily in the coming budget year? Will the practice drop existing contracts and/or pick up new ones? What will be the average charge per visit? How many days per year will the practice be open? What is the estimate for hospital charges and/or procedures? Quantifying the answers to these questions will assist the practice in establishing projected revenue from fee-for-service sources. The Medical Group Management annual surveys can assist in providing a check to make certain revenue estimates appear reasonable.

Another key element in determining the medical practice budget is estimating collections. Obviously, charging for services and receiving payment for those services are two very different things. First, the practice must determine collection percentage based on payor mix (i.e., Medicare, Medicaid, major commercial payors). From this data, the practice can compute its specific goal collection percentage.

For example, assume the practice has the following mix of payors based on charges:

Medicare	30%
Medicaid	10%
Commercial	60%

A review of explanation of benefits (EOBs) from the major payors should be performed to determine reimbursement on the top 20 most-often-performed or highest-dollar-volume of Current Procedural Terminology (CPT) codes for the practice. Exhibit 8.1 is an example spreadsheet setup for this analysis.

Totals of each column should be divided by the group fee to develop the maximum gross collection percentage that each payor could realize if 100 percent of the allowed fee and the patient's copay were collected.

Assume that this analysis yields collection rates on those top 20 codes as follows:

EXHIBIT 8.1
Spreadsheet Setup for Review of EOBs

CPT					OUR	M'CARE	M'CAID	COMM
CODE	DESCRIPTION	VOLUME			FEE	FEE	FEE	FEE

Medicare	55%
Medicaid	50%
Commercial	80%

Knowing the mix and gross collection ratio will allow the practice to compute its goal collection percentage as follows:

	% of Charges		Collection %		
Medicare	30%	×	55%	=	16.5%
Medicaid	10%	×	50%	=	5.0%
Commercial	60%	×	80%	=	40.0%
Goal collection %					61.5%

Based on the above facts, the practice in this scenario should antici-pate a gross collection percentage of 61.5 percent. Once again, the infor-mation included in the MGMA surveys can be used as a sanity check. However, the collection percentage for each practice will vary based on its unique fee structure and payor mix. If the practice has a high fee schedule, the gross collection percentage obviously will be less. Addition-ally, if the practice maintains both a commercial and a Medicare fee schedule (blended fee schedule), the gross collection rate should be higher than that developed from a single fee schedule. Fee schedules de-veloped on a relative value scale provide additional data to assist in rev-enue projections.

In estimating collections, anticipated increases/decreases in reim-bursement also must be considered. For instance, for year 2000, Medicare reimbursement rates are projected to decline by 3 percent for cardiolo-gists. Conversely, family practitioner reimbursement rates are projected to increase by 2 percent. Prepaid revenues should be estimated as a sepa-rate line item on the budget. The fee-for-service equivalent charge for all prepaid patients should not be included in the analysis just described in determining the maximum gross collection percentage of the group. Performance of capitated plans should be analyzed to determine if the upcoming budget should include continued participation. Performance of major managed care contracts should be reviewed. Contracts that provide for a percentage of Medicare fee schedules should be analyzed to determine the impact on the group's financial status. If a plan is a financial drain on the practice, whether to continue to participate in this plan must be considered.

EXPENSES

After budget revenues are established, practice expenses must be projected. The initital step in this process is to separate expenses into fixed and variable. Fixed expenses do not generally vary with patient activity (i.e., rent, salary expense, and utility expense) while variable expenses depend on patient activity (i.e., medical supplies). Historical expenses should be reviewed and compared to established benchmarks, such as the Medical Group Management Association Cost and Production survey. Variable expenses may be established as a percentage of revenue—for example, medical supplies at two percent of revenue with a four percent cost-of-living increase. Opportunities to reduce/control expenses based on a comparison to established benchmarks should be considered as part of the budgeting process. Expenses should be projected based on a best estimate that considers all of these factors. Be sure to include cost-of-living increases and anticipated increases in other expense items (i.e., insurance, postage, maintenance).

The process of gathering all of the information necessary to compile a budget can be tedious, but it is an invaluable discipline. It allows the medical practice to obtain a snapshot view of its successes and its shortcomings regarding revenue, productivity, and allocation of resources. It can help the practice answer such questions as " Do we want to continue our association with a particular managed care payor?" "Do we really need to add another provider/physician?"

Involving the physician group in this process allows physicians to observe, firsthand, how their contribution affects the overall operations of the practice. The budget process can assist the practice in answering questions about changes in compensation levels. Preparing the physician work budget can be an "eye opener" as it reveals existing workloads that may be out of line with existing compensation levels.

CAPITAL BUDGETS

Additionally, capital expenditures and debt acquisition and/or retirement must be considered in budget development. Is new equipment required? Will the new equipment generate new income? What about leasehold improvements? Does the practice want to grow—new offices, staff, and services?

Budget time is also the time to review practice debt. Capital expense and debt are closely connected. Debt can either hold a practice back or fuel its growth. The interest portion of debt is an operating expense. Debt retirement is a decrease to cash flow that does not provide a deductible expense. Refinancing debt can shift cash flow. These decisions can provide the funds to finance practice priorities.

Careful consideration should be given before increasing debt to cover operating expenses. If the practice is growing and needs working capital to fund the increase in expenses until receivables are collected, then debt is a viable alternative for funding. However, if the practice is borrowing simply to maintain physician compensation levels in a declining practice, increasing debt will only add to the downward spiral. The practice must address its current situation realistically and take the actions needed to balance income and expenses. A well-designed budget can assist the practice in reviewing the financial components that will impact such decisions.

Earlier discussions regarding "defining the pie" addressed the issue of profit versus cash. Many groups that have failed to plan appropriately for debt incurred for the acquisition of assets find themselves in a situation at year end whereby there is profit but not an equal amount of cash. With personal service corporations being taxed at the highest corporate tax rate of 35 percent, the group most likely would not want to pay taxes. However, most individuals in the group would not embrace the concept of borrowing cash to pay compensation.

Most groups do not understand the concept of "investing" resources in the practice. Not only are principal payments on debt not deductible, but any new purchases of capital assets using cash from operations creates profit and no cash. What the group must understand is that there are basically two ways of investing in the business, debt or equity. As most groups are not going to issue more stock (equity method of obtaining capital), the standard method of investing is to borrow the funds or finance indirectly by taking reduced compensation. Either option works; however, the method is not always chosen prospectively. Preparing a capital budget annually that takes debt service into consideration will assist the group in developing a compensation pool that more accurately reflects cash.

Establishing a budget for a medical practice is time consuming but necessary, tedious but informative. It is trying but rewarding in terms of keeping a practice on track for goal achievement. Most important, a budget is essential to determine physician compensation appropriately.

DETERMINING BASE

Once the budget is determined, base salary amounts can be established. Base salaries should be competitive based on the specialty and market. They can be demotivating in a group where existing physicians are paid less than new recruits. The MGMA surveys provide compensation amounts by specialty and location that can be used to assist the practice in determining the competitiveness of the base amount.

Base compensation should be established based on the physician achieving certain minimum (core) standards. Those standards may include:

- Tenure: Base salary may be set at differing levels for individuals based on years of service or seniority. Actual hands-on experience usually translates into additional income for the physician and the practice. The MGMA *1999 Report Based on 1998 Data* indicates that physician compensation increases based on years of service. For example, the median compensation for an internal medicine physician with one to two years of experience is $120,810, while internal medicine physicians with three to seven years of experience earn $131,995.

- Qualifications: Consideration can be given in the base salary amount for achieving certain qualifications, such as a board or subspecialty designation.

- Work hours, call rotation: Work standards are necessary to delineate what is expected of a full-time equivalent physician. Work standards provide indices by which to measure physician performance and ensure that behavior is commensurate with group objectives.

   Work hours can be a significant component of the base salary computation, particularly in those situations where physicians desire to reduce their schedules and perhaps work part time. Family and/or health considerations may cause physicians to reduce their patient schedule on either a temporary or a permanent basis. The base salary computation should provide a basis for the minimum work schedule and should be adjusted proportionately for any reduction.

A reduction or elimination in call rotation may, however, create greater concern and dissension within a group practice than a reduction in office time. For instance, a surgeon may request to withdraw from the call schedule one to two years prior to retirement. In many cases, call rotation is worth much more to the remaining members of the group than the reduction in work hours.

The group should define the impact of a withdrawal from the call rotation prior to the request so that all involved may have an equal and impartial vote. One method of resolving this issue is to reverse the situation. A separate pool of funds would be designated as call pay, and only those who are willing to put in the time will participate in this pool.

• Patient volume: In a fee-for-service environment, production drives revenue. In order for a practice to be successful financially, physician members must be committed to seeing patients. In cases of large practice mergers and acquisitions of practices by third parties, the tendency may be for physicians to reduce their schedule. It has been said that the most dangerous financial situation for a practice exists when physicians have the checkbook. On the contrary, when physicians lose the connection between what they produce and the impact on the bottom line, then the practice may be in true financial danger.

The 1999 MGMA report contains data by specialty for ambulatory encounters, hospital encounters, surgery/anesthesia cases, and physician work RVUs. For example, the median ambulatory encounters for an internist is 3,353 (3,584 RVUs). Based on a median of 47 five-day work weeks a year (statistics for work weeks are also included in the MGMA survey), this equates to a median of approximately 14 to15 patient visits per day. In looking at a minimum work schedule for base compensation purposes, perhaps an internal medicine practice would want to consider 15 patients per day to be its minimum work standard.

It is important to make a distinction between production in the form of work schedule and/or ambulatory encounters (or RVUs) and production in the form of dollars. If the standard is set in dollars, physicians might be encouraged to upcode visits. This practice should never be encouraged, and a compliance program should be in place in the group practice to ensure that services performed are appropriately coded according to medical record documentation.

The physician group, however, must be encouraged to comply with agreed-upon work schedules and scheduling parameters. The agreed-upon work schedule can provide the basis of the revenue projections for the practice budget. Physicians should likewise receive routine reports that reflect their visits/schedule as compared to the standard. (A sample report is included in Appendix A.)

Reviewing the physician work schedule/ambulatory encounters likewise will assist the practice in determining the feasibility of adding new physicians. All too often, physician groups make decisions to add new physicians without understanding the financial implications. If physicians in the group are below the standard number of ambulatory visits, then they should give careful consideration to adding another physician in the same specialty.

- Management duties: Employee physicians typically are required to perform nonclinical duties. Those duties may include supervising staff, attending committee or board meetings, and/or participating on hospital committees. If these duties exceed the normal requirements imposed on all physicians (i.e., supervising employees), an additional base amount may be considered.

  Small and medium-size groups typically do not compensate for administrative duties. As long as there is an equal distribution of duties, the group mentality of "sharing" in the management of the practice supports the policy of no additional pay for these services. When these activities become burdensome, the group should consider delegating more of them to the practice manager or hiring additional administrative staff.

  In larger group practices, it is not uncommon for the position of group president, managing partner, or medical director to include administrative time. Most large groups beginning in the late 1990s assigned a physician the responsibility of compliance officer or committee chair. The amount of time devoted to this position may depend on the sophistication of the management group. The group administrator actually may fill the position of chief operating officer, relieving the group president (physician) of day-to-day administrative duties.

A medical group's structure base salary arrangements must be structured in a way that tackles the specific requirements of the group and does not ignore fundamental issues. Defining minimum performance expectations and standards can assist in aligning physician efforts with practice objectives.

The following is a list of sample minimum performance parameters for a primary care physician:

Office hours: Nine four-hour sessions of patient availability, 46 weeks per year.

Quality and cost containment: Nonphysician (indirect) practice expenses that are no more than 52 percent of net medical revenue.

Utilization: Measure based on minimum office visits and hospital admissions, average length of stay, ancillary tests and procedures.

Referral patterns: Measure based on outside referrals.

Patient satisfaction: Measure based on individual physician scores on patient-satisfaction surveys relative to the average physician's score.

CHAPTER NINE

Incentive Compensation

You Get What You Pay For

Incentive compensation is the component of the compensation model that can be designed to direct physician behavior. Properly structured, incentive compensation can challenge physicians to reach the performance levels necessary for group success. Whereas base pay compensates physicians for established minimum standards, incentive pay rewards for service beyond the minimum work standard.

Incentive compensation is usually the contingent portion of the compensation plan and is tied to physicians completing certain performance goals. The incentive piece challenges physicians to reach higher levels of performance and can motivate individual physicians to work toward organizational effectiveness.

For an incentive compensation model to be effective, however, the group must define its strategy. Overall goals must be established and the direction of the group must be defined. The successful incentive system includes developing clear, objective performance expectations and regularly measuring and communicating actual performance compared to target levels. The establishment of a strategic plan is essential for the development of a properly designed incentive plan.

Objectives of the incentive plan may include the following:

- Align physician incentives with group goals and objectives. The goals and intentions of a practice may say one thing, but the physicians could be paid to do something else. Remember, you get what you pay for.

- Encourage productivity while encouraging cost-efficient care. Production drives revenue. In a highly concentrated managed care environment, production must be linked with the appropriate use of resources.

- Control expenses. Managed care revenues (including discounted fee-for-service revenues) have taken control of the top line in medical practices. In order to maintain profits, physicians must control expenses.

- Facilitate the recruitment and retention of high-quality physicians. The incentive plan must provide benefits for physicians who excel in practice. Otherwise, the practice will not be able to attract or retain the best and the brightest.

- Monitor patient satisfaction. Responses to patient surveys, accessibility of physician to patients, adequacy of patient education, patient complaint analysis, and patient retention rates are all gauges that can be used to determine patient satisfaction.

- Provide quality of care. Quality provides a competitive edge. Quality-based premiums in the future may direct patients to practices that demonstrate better performance or quality improvement.

- Reward team effort in addition to individual volume. Assigning a portion of the incentive pay to overall group performance in excess of budget fosters a team mentality in the practice.

- Reward attributes that enhance the goals of the practice (entrepreneurial efforts). The incentive system should incorporate and reward achievements that promote the goals and objectives of the organization.

With the changes occurring in the healthcare industry, many groups are discovering that their traditional methods of measuring performance are no longer aligned with their cultures or business strategies. As groups grow and/or merge with other groups, incentive plans must be adapted to promote the success of the new structures. Increases in managed care likewise may cause a group to look toward new incentives.

In a fee-for-service environment, productivity continues to drive revenue. A recent survey conducted by the CPA Health Care Advisors Association indicated that of the 124 medical practices surveyed, 95 percent considered productivity to be the number-one factor in determining physician compensation. In the MGMA *1999 Report Based on 1998 Data*, 39.28 percent of the medical practices surveyed reported that either gross charges or adjusted charges were used in the compensation methodology. Primary care physicians included in the survey indicated that 33.79 percent of their compensation methodology was based 100 percent on productivity. The corresponding percentage for specialists was 30.23 percent.

The correlation between production and compensation is changing, according to the MGMA survey. From 1992 to 1995, primary care physicians realized a greater increase in compensation than was evidenced by a corresponding increase in production. For instance, in 1992, compensation to primary care physicians rose by 7.47 percent while production increased only by 2.92 percent. The years 1992 to 1995 coincide with the advent of the "gatekeeper" concept and the push by multispecialty groups and other healthcare providers to lock in primary care referral sources. A major factor in the increase in compensation was the corresponding increase in reimbursement due to the implementation of the resource-based relative value scale (RBRVS) fee schedule, discussed in Chapter 2. The result was an increase in compensation beyond the corresponding increase in productivity.

The increase in primary care compensation during the mid-1990s could be viewed, in part, as a market correction, as primary care salaries had long been well below those of their specialist counterparts. The result, however, created a disincentive to production in many cases, which caused negative financial implications to merging multispecialty groups and acquiring entities (i.e., hospitals, physician practice management companies). In the late 1990s, the trend in compensation to production for primary care reversed. From 1997 to 1998, primary care compensation increased by 2.54 percent as compared to a 4.67 percent increase in production.

Incentive compensation must be designed to promote the desired behavior. As with the example of the primary care physicians, an ill-designed plan can create financial disasters. Group incentives must be designed to align incentives and position the group for success.

Obviously, *productivity* must be included as a primary incentive factor. As managed care pentrates further into a group practice, the need for other performance factors may likewise increase. As new goals, objectives, and expectations develop, incentives must be created to achieve them.

Patient base growth may be considered as an incentive component. Growth is measured in new patient visits or an increase in enrollment.

Resource management becomes an increasingly important factor in a period of declining reimbursement. Managed care and the Medicare/Medicaid programs currently control approximately 74 percent of total group practice revenues. Financial success, in many cases, depends on how well the group is able to control expenses and manage resources.

The development of departmental cost budgets provides the group practice with goals upon which incentives can be developed. For instance, consideration could be given in the incentive formula to the management of departmental resources within budget. Alternatively, the budget could provide a basic cost per RVU upon which a portion of incentive compensation could be based.

Patient satisfaction becomes an important performance factor in a competitive market. With declining reimbursement and an increase in managed care, physicians may lose sight of patient satisfaction due to financial pressures. The implementation of Health Plan Employer Data and Information Set (HEDIS) guidelines about satisfaction surveys encourages groups to become proactive in surveying patients before the government and managed care does it for them. The physician who is habitually late for appointments should not be rewarded for this behavior but rather should be given an incentive to be timely.

An objective patient survey will assist in determining patients' independent perspectives of care. The survey results can be used as a factor in determining incentive pay.

Quality measures, such as outcomes management, may be more difficult to quantify. To some degree, patient satisfaction surveys provide a measure of quality of care from patients' perspectives. Other quality goals may be developed by the group (i.e., number of inpatient days per 1,000 patients), and incentives can be designed accordingly. Incentives likewise may be assigned to the degree of compliance with protocols and guidelines.

Overall efficiency measures the group's overall success. Efficiency is measured in terms of contribution to margin for purposes of the incentive. A portion of the incentive could be allocated to the group based on the achievement of a projected profit.

Gainsharing is a term that carries negative implications due to recent pronouncements against hospital incentives to physicians by the Office of the Inspector General (OIG) of the United States Department of Health and Human Services. Civil monetary penalties (CMP law) for up to $2,000 per patient can be imposed on hospitals and physicians for making or receiving "a payment, directly or indirectly, to a physician as an inducement to reduce or limit services provided with respect to individuals who (1) are entitled to Medicare or Medicaid benefits and (2) are under the care of the physician." Because the CMP law expressly applies to hospital payments intended to induce physicians to reduce or limit services to .

Medicare and Medicaid patients, physician group incentive plans that reward cost savings remain permissible, as long as services provided to Medicare and Medicaid patients are not affected. Compensation under any physician incentive plan should be based on positive quality assurance outcomes. Patient care cannot be compromised through financial incentives designed to control costs.

The CMP law does "not apply to hospital incentive arrangements with physicians who have a management or supervisory responsibility with respect to the operation of hospital departments (such as radiology or clinical laboratory services) insofar as the purpose of the arrangement is limited to encouraging efficiency in the operation of the department" (House Report No. 99-727, p. 445). For instance, rewarding physicians, such as pathologists or radiologists, for efficient department operations may be permissible, as long as the incentive arrangement does not apply to those physicians with direct patient care responsibilities.

Additionally, hospitals may pay physicians fixed fees for consulting-like services directed at reducing hospital costs. Hospitals may align incentives with physicians to achieve cost savings through personal service contracts where hospitals pay physicians based on a fixed fee that is fair market value for services rendered, rather than a percentage of cost savings. Payment of fees can in no way be contingent upon attaining projected cost savings.

Physicians likewise may be paid a fixed fee for their participation on committees formed to develop initiatives to reduce hospital costs. The fees paid may be based on projected savings but cannot be contingent on achieving projected savings.

Based on the above, hospitals and physicians must be cautious in structuring incentive programs that include rewards for cost savings. Existing agreements must be reviewed in light of the OIG's position on gainsharing. Although the OIG is not offering amnesty for terminating existing agreements, it will give consideration to entities that expeditiously terminate noncompliant plans.

Until 1987, the Internal Revenue Service took a very restrictive view, finding incentive compensation plans for tax-exempt organizations based on any interest in net profits to be prohibited (GCM 35869). In 1987 (GCM 39670, October 14, 1987), the IRS reversed its historic position and approved the payment of deferred compensation, together with the actual income earned thereon from the date of the deferrals. Service approval of profit-sharing incentive compensation plans (including for executives) is based on the economic performance of the organization in those cases in which there is a cap on what is paid and the maximum that can be paid, together with all other compensation, is reasonable (GCM 39674).

The IRS has found acceptable incentive compensation for tax-exempt entities complying with the following factors:

- The contractual relationship is completely arm's length, preferably with the service provider having no participation in the management or control of the organization.

- The contingent payments serve a real and discernible business purpose of the exempt organization independent of any purpose to operate the organization for the direct or indirect benefit of the service provider (achieving maximum efficiency and economy in operations by shifting away the principal risk of operating cost to the service provider so as to alleviate the organization's need to carry a large insurance-type reserve).

- The amount of compensation is not dependent principally on incoming revenue of the exempt organization but rather on the accomplishment of the objectives of the compensatory contract (the success of the employer organization and the service provider in keeping actual expenses within the limits of projected expenses on which the ultimate prices of charitable services are based).

- Review of the actual operating results reveals no evidence of abuse or unwarranted benefits (prices and operating costs compare favorably with those of other similar organizations).

- The presence of a ceiling or reasonable maximum so as to avoid the possibility of a windfall benefit to the service provider based on factors bearing no direct relationship to the level of service provided.

Incentive compensation based on the services personally performed by the recipient is the least likely type of incentive to raise problems. Incentive compensation that rewards the recipient for performance in an area where the recipient performed no significant personal or supervisory services may be viewed as prohibited sharing of the organization's net profits. It is always useful to have an incentive component based on contributions to the mission statement, quality of service, and public satisfaction, not simply the bottom line.

In order for incentive compensation to provide the desired motivational results, it must be understood and accepted as fair by members of the physician group. An overly complex formula can not direct behavior. Physicians must understand the impact that certain behaviors and actions will have on their compensation.

When designing or refining an incentive plan, the physician group should review the projected results before the plan is instituted. For instance, the formula could be applied to historical or projected earnings to determine if the proposed model achieves the desired financial results prior to initiation. Buy-in of the physician group is essential to the success of the plan.

CHAPTER TEN

Physician Benefit Plans

A major, although often neglected, component of the physician compensation model is an allocation for employee benefits. Benefit plans can comprise a significant portion of the total compensation package and typically provide the physician with tax-free benefits.

Typically, the package of benefits is uniform across the physician group. The cost of the benefit packages (i.e., retirement plan contributions), however, may differ by physician and should be taken into account in the total physician cost. Often physician benefits are accounted for in the compensation model as a direct expense to the physician.

Benefit plans typically include the following:

- Health insurance: Group health insurance is a benefit that is comparable for all employees within the practice. A differential, however, may exist with the physician group if dependent coverage is provided.

- Qualified retirement plans: Retirement plan contributions for physicians can constitute a significant benefit. The amount of the plan contribution will vary based on the individual physician's wages and/or age. A properly designed retirement plan can provide significant pre-tax benefits to the physicians and can provide for long-term financial security. Careful plan design also can allow for a cost-efficient contribution for employees while maximizing the physician's contribution.

- Life insurance: Group term life insurance (death benefit below $50,000) may be offered to all employees as a tax-free benefit (typically offered as an adjunct to the health insurance plan). Physicians likewise may be insured by the corporation under key-man policies to provide for buyouts in the event of death.

- Disability insurance: Most physicians consider disability insurance to be a valuable benefit. Long-term disability insurance is designed to protect physicians against financial hardship resulting from extended illness or injury. Physicians often enhance their employer's policy with a disability policy from a professional organization.

  Choosing a policy requires careful analysis. The policy should be reviewed based on the disability benefit provided, the definition of disability, any benefit offsets, the benefit duration, portability, survivor benefit, and availability of cost-of-living increases.

  Disability insurance can be provided as a tax-free benefit if it is provided for employee physicians in a professional corporation (C corporation) or a professional association. Disability insurance premium payments will vary depending on the individual physician's salary and age.

- Cafeteria plans: Cafeteria plans can provide both physician and staff benefits. Through cafeteria plans, employees (including the physicians) can elect salary deferrals from a "menu" of pretax benefits. The benefits can include medical reimbursement benefits (including dependent health coverage), disability insurance, and dependent child care benefits. Elections must be made annually, and the plan may not discriminate in favor of the owner-employees (i.e., physicians).

- Vacation benefits: Vacation benefits may vary depending on the physician's tenure with the practice. Group practices typically provide three to six weeks in vacation benefits for employees. Likewise, practices may offer sabbaticals on a rotation basis. Available vacation and sabbatical leave must be considered in developing revenue projections, by physician, for budget purposes.

- Continuing medical education: Group practices must provide physician members with adequate time off (typically 40 hours per year) to fulfill continuing medical education (CME) requirements. Annual allowances (i.e., $2,500 per physician) typically are set to provide for travel costs and tuition.

- Professional fees and dues: The group practice typically is responsible for all license fees. The practice may set limits (by physician) for other professional dues and subscriptions.

- Expense allowances: The group may provide the physician members with other miscellaneous benefits including cellular phones and automobile usage reimbursement. Limits may be set, per physician, for these benefits. In some cases, groups will assign an expense allowance amount to each physician as a maximum amount for expense reimbursement. This type of plan should provide a list of expenses that can be presented for reimbursement. In order for the practice to deduct the reimbursement, it must be for an ordinary and necessary business expense.

Retirement plan contributions made by the practice on behalf of the physician employee typically constitute the greatest tax-deferred benefit both in dollar amount paid by the practice and financial reward to the physician. A qualified pension plan provides systematically for the payment of definitely determinable benefits to employees (and their beneficiaries) after retirement over a period of years, usually for life. Retirement benefits generally are measured by such factors as years of the employee's service and compensation received. Benefits under a defined benefit plan are "definitely determinable" if they are determined actuarially, on a basis that precludes employer discretion. Defined contribution plans, on the other hand, provide for contributions based on a fixed formula. Current tax law (year 2000) permits the practice to contribute up to $30,000 per year to defined contribution plans (25 percent of compensation up to $170,000) on behalf of a physician.

Our tax system allows us to encourage physicians to do that which they might not do otherwise. Tax breaks are given to encourage retirement savings.

For a qualified plan:

- Contributions are tax deductible
- Investment earnings are tax deferred
- Assets are protected from creditors

To prevent abuse, the tax code places limitations and restrictions on retirement plans receiving favorable tax treatments. These limitations and restrictions are generally intended to prevent plans from discriminating in favor of owners and other highly paid employees. For example, a plan cannot cover the physician-owners and exclude all other employees.

Basically, plans cannot discriminate in favor of "highly compensated employees (HCEs)." HCEs are employees who either:

- Earn over $85,000 per year (effective in 2000)
- Own more than 5 percent of the practice

Certain employees can be excluded from coverage. Those employees include:

- Employees under the age of twenty-one
- Employees who have less than one (or two) years of service
- Highly compensated employees (HCEs)

Additionally, the 70 percent rule states that the percentage of non-HCEs a plan covers must be equal to or greater than 70 percent of the percentage of HCEs covered. For example, if a practice has 2 physicians (HCEs) and 10 employees (non-HCEs), the plan may:

- Cover all the employees (non-HCEs)
- Cover at least 7 non-HCEs

Qualified plans are not free from costs. There are administrative costs to establish qualified plans that vary based on plan type and complexity. Additionally, there are the costs of funding for the retirement benefits of nonowner employees.

Qualified plans must provide that a participant's right to his or her accrued benefit vests at certain rates during the years of his or her employment. Benefits derived from employee contributions (i.e., 401(k) plans) must be 100 percent vested at all times. Benefits derived from employer contributions must become nonforfeitable when the employee reaches normal retirement age (the later of age 65 or the fifth anniversary of participation in the plan).

A "top-heavy" plan must meet additional requirements in the area of vesting. Most group practice plans will be top heavy (majority of retirement benefits going to the owner-employee). In a top-heavy plan, the employee's right to accrued benefits must be 100 percent vested after three years of service or, at the employer's option, 20 percent vested after two years' service and 20 percent in each of the following years (100 percent vested after six years of service).

Retirement savings in a tax-deferred retirement plan may provide the bulk of the physician's retirement. For example, an annual contribution of $30,000 earning 8 percent will grow to over $3,600,000 in 30 years. The consideration for the physician, however, is "Will this be enough?"

Life insurance company studies indicate that the life expectancy of a couple with an attained age of 35 is 89.0 years old. Furthermore, if the couples have excellent health (no heart disease, uncontrolled high blood pressure, diabetes, cancer, or other abnormal conditions), in nearly 30 percent of the cases, one member of the couple will still be alive at age 95.

The following list indicates the lump-sum amount that would be needed to provide inflation-adjusted spendable (after-tax) income of

$100,000 per year for varying terms (assuming 8 percent return, average post–World War II inflation, tax rate of 35 percent):

Term	Lump Sum Needed
20 years	$2,030,000
25 years	$2,340,000
30 years	$2,600,000

As we learn more about the latest research on longevity and life expectancies and how much longer people are living than was previously thought, it is essential to review this chart and reevaluate the number of years that might be needed to be planned for in retirement. Assuming a retirement age of 65 in good health, a physician might live for 25 or 30 years in retirement.

For a physician to maintain at least $100,000 annually in postretirement earnings (after tax) for 30 years, as indicated above, the plan should have approximately $2,600,000 in lump-sum assets available at retirement. This would require 26.5 years of consistent annual contributions of $30,000 per year (assuming an 8 percent return). It is imperative that physicians establish plans early and fund consistently in order to provide for retirement.

Defined contribution plans include money purchase plans, where the contribution is fixed each year, and profit-sharing plans, in which the contribution is flexible. A money purchase plan will allow for a contribution up to 25 percent of covered compensation (currently $170,000) while the limit on profit-sharing contributions is 15 percent of compensation. For top-heavy plans, the employer must contribute for each nonkey employee not less than 3 percent of that employee's compensation. The percentage, however, does not have to exceed the percentage at which contributions are made or required to be made for the key employees with the highest contribution percentage. A defined contribution plan provides for periodic contributions to be made into each participant's account. The accounts are invested and the participants' benefit depends on how the account grows.

Many practices will opt for a combination of the two plans. For instance, a money purchase plan can be set up with a contribution of 10 percent along with a profit-sharing plan that will allow for a 15 percent contribution. By combining the two plans, the practice will be able to reach the 25 percent maximum; however, only the 10 percent money purchase contribution will be fixed each year. The profit-sharing contribution is flexible and can be funded up to 15 percent or not at all, depending on the financial situation of the practice.

Employers often favor defined contribution plans. These plans are relatively easy to understand because each employee has his or her own individual account that grows with contributions and investment earnings each year. However, the Internal Revenue Code places relatively low limits on the amounts that can be contributed on behalf of owners and other highly paid employees under these defined contribution plans.

Defined benefit plans allow the practice to fund for a benefit at retirement not to exceed the lesser of 100 percent of the highest three years' compensation or the index amount (currently $130,000). Top-heavy plans must provide a minimum annual retirement benefit, not integrated with social security, for a nonkey employee equal to the lesser of: (1) 2 percent of the participant's average compensation for years in the testing period multiplied by his or her years of service with the employer or (2) 20 percent of his or her average compensation in the years in the testing period. There is no limit on the dollar amount of contribution to a defined benefit plan, as plan funding is based on actuarial determinations to provide a benefit at retirement. An actuary determines contributions so that there will be enough money in the plan to pay the specified benefit. Additionally, beginning in the year 2000, there are no special limitations for participating in both a defined contribution and a defined benefit plan.

Certain other plans may provide benefits for the owner-employees (physicians) while limiting the cost of providing benefits to rank-and-file employees. A combination of plans incorporating a 401(k) plan that allows for employee deferrals may help to defray costs.

Defined benefit plans may be attractive for practices that have an age differential between the physician-employees and the staff. Since defined benefit plans fund for a benefit at retirement based on current earnings and years to retirement, the contribution may be maximized for the older employee group since there are fewer years to retirement.

One alternative to pension funding is a cash balance plan. A cash balance plan is like a profit-sharing plan that credits a specified rate of return to participants' accounts. Cash balance plans retain the simplicity of the individual account approach but are not considered to be defined contribution plans. Thus they can allow much larger contributions.

Exhibit 10.1 shows the maximum annual contribution available for participants of varying ages.

With a cash balance plan, an account is established for each participant. Contributions are made to each account in accordance with a formula specified in the plan. The plan usually is set up so that the owners and other key employees receive the maximum possible benefit. Contributions for nonkey employees usually are expressed as a percentage of pay, for example, 5 percent. Nondiscrimination tests must be passed to

EXHIBIT 10.1
Minimum Annual Contribution—Cash Balance Plan

Age	Cash Balance Limit	Defined Contribution Limit
30	$23,000	$30,000 in all years
35	29,400	
40	37,600	
45	51,900	
50	66,400	
55	85,000	
60	108,800	
65	149,200	

ensure that contributions do not discriminate in favor of highly compensated employees. The services of an actuary must be used to determine the annual contribution.

The plan provides that each participant's account will be credited with a specified rate of interest. When participants terminate employment, they take their vested account balance with them, just as in a defined contribution plan. Account balances can be transferred to an IRA or another qualified plan to defer taxes.

Although cash balance plans are more complex to operate that traditional defined contribution plans, they can be a useful way to accumulate funds for retirement. Similar benefits (age, compensation) can be obtained with target benefit plans. Target benefit plan contributions fund for a retirement benefit based on the age of the participant and the participant's compensation. However, the annual contribution limits are similar to defined contribution plans (currently a $30,000 annual contribution per participant). With a target benefit plan, the practice can benefit the older physician group while controlling costs.

Retirement plan contributions can provide not only for long-term financial security for the physicians but also a benefit for staff that can increase retention. Careful plan design likewise can allow the practice to provide benefits while minimizing overall cost. Since retirement plan design is determined by the current tax law, it is imperative that current laws be reviewed in designing new plans and in keeping existing plans in compliance.

Insurance planning through the practice can provide benefits for the physicians as well as the practice. As mentioned previously, the incorporated practice can provide up to $50,000 term life insurance on a nondiscriminatory basis and deduct the cost of the insurance as a fringe benefit.

Additionally, the practice can provide disability insurance as a deductible fringe benefit.

Financial security for the practice and the physician may include the provision of life insurance and disability insurance. Life and/or disability insurance proceeds can provide for the redemption of the physician-owner's interest in the practice. Additionally, insurance proceeds can provide the practice with benefits to cover the loss of income generated by the departing physician.

Group life insurance plans usually require no proof of insurability, and benefits are typically a multiple of base salary. The average multiple is two to three times the base salary. The group plan likewise may provide the right to convert the group term insurance to an individual policy at termination of employment, again without proof of insurability. This becomes a valuable benefit to physicians who, because of advanced age or poor health, would not otherwise be able to obtain life insurance.

Plans such as split-dollar life insurance can provide a buyout benefit for the physician's interest while providing a benefit to the practice to provide for the loss of income incurred. Split-dollar life insurance is an agreement in which the benefits and the costs of a life insurance policy are split between the employer and the physician. Cash-value life insurance rather that term insurance is used for this type of plan. Before implementing this type of plan, a careful analysis of the tax implications to the practice and the physician should be performed.

Disability buyout plans can provide a benefit for the physician who withdraws from the practice due to disability. Through a disability buyout policy, the practice can financially insure for an unexpected buyout liability.

Nonqualified plans may be established to supplement physician retirement. Such plans may be funded or nonfunded. A nonfunded plan may simply provide for salary continuation to the physician for a period of time at retirement.

Funded plans allow an entity to make contributions to a trustee or an insurance company on behalf of an individual. To avoid immediate taxation on these contributions, there has to be a "substantial risk of forfeiture" surrounding these funds. When this risk is removed, the recipient is considered to be in constructive receipt of these contributions and is taxed immediately on the entire amount. Therefore, the physician may face a dilemma. Either the accumulating benefit is at risk or a significant tax bill may be due by the physician. Additionally, the contributions made by the practice to a funded nonqualified plan are not tax deductible. With a flat rate of 35 percent for personal service corporations, tax implications may impact the decision to maintain a funded plan.

CHAPTER ELEVEN

Measuring Productivity

Productivity is an important component of the physician compensation model. In the eat-what-you-kill model, productivity (translated into cash collections) defines compensation. As part of an incentive plan, productivity continues to be given significant weight as an important component for financial success (especially in the fee-for-service environment).

An integral part of the physician compensation model lies in the definition of productivity. Productivity may be defined as gross charges, net charges, collections, relative value units (RVUs), or some internally developed unit of measure (points). In all cases, the definition of productivity assigned to the physician in the compensation formula may not include their direct referrals to designated health services (Stark II). Each definition has pros and cons that must be weighed carefully before utilizing it as a basis for allocating income in the compensation process.

GROSS CHARGES

Gross charges are defined as the total production (volume times fee) assigned to the physician for the compensation period. One benefit of using gross charges to define productivity is that the amounts are readily accessible in most electronic medical billing systems. The information is available and is generally understood and accepted as a fair representation of the total work performed by each physician. According to the Medical Group Management Association 1999 Report, 24 percent of the survey respondents used gross charges to measure productivity.

Gross charges, however, may have no correlation to cash collections. Using gross charges as an indicator of productivity may misrepresent the individual physician's contribution to the bottom line.

Additionally, gross charges may not represent the physician's work effort. In mature practices, the fee schedule may have evolved haphazardly over time with no relation to work units or RVUs. The group may use multiple fee schedules to record charge volume (i.e., a separate fee schedule for Medicare and non-Medicare patients). An ill-defined fee schedule can distort individual productivity measured by gross charge volume.

Another factor that tends to skew work effort based on charges is the case mix for different specialists. This issue exists for both single-specialty and multispecialty groups. Take, for example, an orthopedic group. Physicians performing back surgeries rather than specializing in foot or hand care will produce higher charges. Do the physicians agree that, based on her production, the back surgeon has expended more time and skill to provide those services? Cardiology provides another example. Invasive specialists produce higher charge dollars and conversely would not expect to pay as much for overhead as they spend most of their time in the hospital setting with little clinic time. These are situations whereby a group mentality would support a sharing of revenues in order to provide not only cardiology procedures but also the consultative, diagnostic, and follow-up care required for patients with cardiac disease.

Another advantage to using gross charges based on one fee schedule is that payor mix is not a factor. It is a group decision that no one physician should be penalized based on his or her accepting more Medicaid or other patients covered by contractually accepted low reimbursement. An example would be the pediatrician in a multispecialty group who sees a higher percentage of Medicaid patients that may generate a high level of charges at a low collection percentage. Again, it should be a group decision and agreement that the work effort of these physicians is equal to that of those physicians who do not accept Medicaid.

As the fee schedule serves as the "conversion factor" for charges, it is important that group members understand what that factor is and how it was developed. They must agree that this conversion factor is a fair representation of their work effort.

ADJUSTED CHARGES

The MGMA cost and production survey reported that 14.90 percent of respondents use adjusted charges to define productivity in compensation models. Adjusted charges represent gross charges that have been adjusted for contractual write-offs and estimated bad debts.

In using adjusted charges, an attempt is made to adjust gross charges to anticipated collections. The benefit exists in the fact that the data used represent the current productivity for the period. Collections, on the other hand, may represent reimbursement for productivity not included in the compensation period.

The downside to using adjusted gross charges to define productivity exists in the fact that the adjustments applied to gross charges are a best estimate of collections. Any estimates used in the compensation calculations may lead to speculation. Administrative staff and systems may not provide adequate data to determine accurately the contractual write-off estimates. An analysis of adjusted gross charges would indicate that the result is an expectation of collections if the entity could, in fact, be paid in the same month the service is provided. Therefore, unless the group can implement the system to develop and administer this measure of productivity in a cost-effective manner, the alternative method of collections would seem appropriate.

COLLECTIONS

Cash is king.
—Unknown

Most group practices use total collections (net medical revenue) on physician gross charges to measure productivity. In the 1999 MGMA cost and production survey, 46 percent of the respondents used collections to define productivity in the compensation methodology.

Collections are easily defined and readily accessible in the group practice management data. Additionally, collections relate directly to the bottom-line financial results for the compensation period.

Collections, however, may not relate specifically to the production generated during the compensation period. In most medical practices, the average turnaround on collections is 60 days. Additionally, collections may be distorted based on payor mix. If a physician is allocated a disproportionate share of Medicaid patients, for example, his or her collections may be disproportionately below production.

An inherent problem in measuring productivity based on collections is that the physician generally has no control over the collection results. System problems, people problems, and payor problems generally do not come to the attention of the physician until collections have bottomed out. Reporting mechanisms must be in place to keep physicians informed of any problems arising that ultimately will affect take-home pay. Administrators and office managers must play an active role in the accounts receivable function in order to provide physicians with a level of comfort that the system is working to their advantage.

RELATIVE VALUE UNITS

Relative value units (RVUs) may be applied to charge data to measure productivity. Relative value units, associated with Medicare's Resource Based Relative Value Scale (RBRVS), is the system of assigning units to Current Procedural Terminology (CPT) codes that in recent years has been adopted by most third-party payors as well as physician practices, to develop and maintain fee schedules. RVUs, as defined by the Medicare RBRVS, assign a unit to each service provided (CPT code) based on the physician work effort, practice expense factor, and malpractice amount.

RVUs allow the practice to measure productivity in a method that is not distorted by an ill-defined fee schedule or affected by a bad payor mix. The downside to using RVUs may result in the calculation. Many practice management systems are not set up to express the work performed (CPT codes) in relative value units. If the system cannot automatically convert production to RVUs, a spreadsheet must be developed to perform the calculation. Chapter 12 discusses RVUs in detail.

WEIGHTED AVERAGE PRODUCTION

Some groups utilize an individual production index to calculate production credit. This index usually includes a small base salary and incentive based on the production credit. A production credit index might appear as follows:

Actual Personal Production	% Credit
0–200K	40%
200K–300K	50%
300K–400K	60%
400K–600K	70%
600K or more	80%

Production first would be defined and then indexed according to the established index of the group. Income would be allocated based on this weighted production credit.

POINTS SYSTEM

In the points system, certain percentages of income would be allocated to various categories, such as production, administration, marketing, ownership, number of patient visits, increased number of new patients, call hours worked, and seniority. For example, a pool would be allocated to production at 60 percent of net income. Each physician would be allocated a pro rata portion of the production pool based on either his or her percentage of charges or collections to the total. This system can become cumbersome if the categories' points are assigned to increase continuously.

OTHER METHODS

If all else fails, many groups will develop their own system of measuring productivity. In an effort to have a meeting of the minds on the equivalent work effort, some type of value assignment to each CPT code is necessary. One method is to assign "minutes" to services. Minutes replace RVUs as a measure of work effort and time. Regardless of the nomenclature, what is important is that the physicians believe that each service has been given consideration and is respected for the skill and time required to provide it. These systems can be difficult to administer but may be well worth the cost if group members believe they are a fair representation of work effort.

CHAPTER TWELVE

Relative Value Units

The Medicare RBRVS fee schedule represents the first major change in the way physicians are paid since they stopped accepting chickens and pigs.
—Representative Pete Stark

Relative value units (RVUs) and the resource-based relative value scale (RBRVS) are not new concepts. Actually, the use of relative values in computing physician reimbursement began in California in the 1950s. Initially, the California relative value units (California Standard Nomenclature; CRVS) developed by the California Medical Association were represented by a three-digit code. As technology progressed and new procedures were developed, the code was lengthened to five digits.

Concern developed following initial studies regarding RVUs. Government regulators were concerned that physician association development of relative values could lead to price fixing. In 1976 the Federal Trade Commission used its authority to stop publication of the CRVS because it appeared that the California Medical Association might be found guilty of price fixing as a professional association. In 1979 the U.S. government contested the development and dissemination of a relative value study by a group of physicians (*United States v. American Associates of Anesthesiologists*, 473F. Supp. 147 (1979)). The court upheld that the study was lawful as a methodology in determining fees. For many years, however, studies were curtailed and the only RVU information available was maintained by the large insurers and was unavailable to practitioners.

Many consider the Relative Values for Physicians (RVPs) system to be the most accurate and comprehensive relative-value system. Initially published by McGraw-Hill in 1984, most private insurance payors established fee schedules utilizing RVP until 1992, with the advent of the Medicare RBRVS.

In 1985 the Health Care Financing Administration (HCFA) contracted with Harvard University's School of Public Health to conduct a relative value study. The purpose of the study was to establish the amount of physician work that was involved in performing the services or procedures represented by 7,000 Current Procedural Terminology (CPT) codes.

The university team, led by William C. Hsiao, Ph.D., chose 20 to 24 services in each specialty for which it set relative values. The services chosen were those most frequently performed within each specialty and included a variety of diagnostic, evaluation and management, and invasive services. A description of each service was developed, and a survey was conducted involving a random sample of 3,200 physicians. In the survey, physicians were asked to rate the amount of time, technical skill, and mental and physical effort that would be needed to perform the service described. Additionally, they were asked to rate the stress on the physician associated with providing the service or procedure.

From the survey, individual estimates of work were averaged. Pre- and postwork amounts were estimated and combined with the actual service to determine a single scale of work per service per specialty. Since each specialty estimated work on its own scale, the researchers aligned the specialty scales into a common scale by linking equivalent services performed in common across the specialties. For instance, evaluation and management services were a common link as most all specialties provide these services.

Approximately 400 pairs of services were identified as links during the first phase. The specific values assigned to the links were derived through a regression analysis that identified the most appropriate set of linking values. Once a standard value was assigned to the linking service, the researchers had a point of reference from which to place values on other specialty services.

Obviously, all 7,000 CPT codes were not surveyed. Estimating techniques were used to extrapolate the surveyed service values to those services that were not surveyed. An estimating example included the review of historical charge values in comparison to survey values.

The estimating techniques used resulted in some obvious invalid values. A panel of 200 physician consultants was assembled to review and refine the values assigned to surgical services.

Authorized by a 1989 law, the national physician fee schedule payment system was instituted as a basis for reimbursement in 1992 with full implementation planned for 2001. The aims of the movement to a relative-based scale were to establish a logical method of reimbursement and to slow the rise in spending for physician services.

The previous method of reimbursement was based on a Medicare fee schedule that was adjusted each year based on the customary, prevailing, and reasonable rates of a geographical region. As fees increased, spending increased proportionately. Additionally, increases were not based on any logical work value but primarily on what the market would tolerate.

The RBRVS system is based on a calculation that considers five factors:

1. The time it takes the typical physician to provide a service or perform a procedure
2. The difficulty of the service or procedure
3. The specific geographic area and the related cost of living for the specific area
4. Practice overhead costs in the specific geographic area
5. The cost of malpractice insurance

The five components are combined into a payment formula:

$$\text{Payment} = [\underset{\text{WORK}}{(RVUw \times GPCIw)} + \underset{\text{+ PRACTICE EXPENSE}}{(RVUpe \times GPCIpe)} + \underset{\text{+ MALPRACTICE}}{(RVUm \times GPCIm)}] \times CF$$

where

CF = Uniform national *conversion factor* dollar amount that converts RVUs into a payment amount

$RVUw$ = Physician *work relative value* units for the service

$GPCIw$ = *Geographic practice cost index* value reflecting one-quarter of the geographic variance in physician work applicable in the specific area.

$RVUpe$ = *Physician expense* relative value units for the service; expense units are assigned separately for nonfacility services (i.e., physician office) and facility services (i.e., hospital, ambulatory surgery center, skilled nursing facility)

$GPCIpe$ = *Geographic practice cost index value for practice expense* applicable to the specific fee schedule area to account for regional differences in income, overhead, and professional liability

$RVUm$ = Cost of *malpractice* insurance

$GPCIm$ = *Geographic practice cost index value for malpractice* expense applicable to the fee schedule area

WORK RVUs

Work RVUs account for approximately 55 percent of the physician's total payment under RBRVS. The work component of the RVU calculation represents the average work done by a physician of average efficiency in performing a service.

The global patient service is encompassed in the total work component which includes three components:

1. Intraservices (direct physician interaction)
2. Preservices
3. Postservices

The work component considers the following physician effort in determining a value:

- Time needed to perform the service
- Mental effort and judgement
- Technical skill
- Physical effort
- Stress involved in delivering the care

For example, in 2000 the work RVU for a mid-level (level III) established office visit (CPT code 99213) equals 0.67. The work RVU for repair of a ruptured aortic aneurysm (CPT code 35082) is 36.35. In other words, the work RVUs for these two services indicate that the time, effort, skill, and stress involved in performing an aortic aneurysm repair is approximately 54 times the time, effort, skill, and stress involved in providing a mid-level established office visit.

Work RVUs are reviewed by the HCFA on an annual basis. The annual review exists to primarily assign work RVUs to new services, however, RVUs for existing services may be reviewed as well.

The following four procedures are used for updating work RVUs:

1. Proposed changes to existing RVUs and/or RVUs for new procedures or services are announced in the spring or summer *Federal Register*.
2. A 60 to 90 day public comment period exists that allows for provider opinions and/or concerns to be voiced.
3. After the comment period, the agency publishes final RVU changes in December to become effective in January.
4. In the fall of each year, HCFA assigns interim RVUs to codes for which the CPT code definition has changed. Interim codes likewise may be made permanent the following January, after public comments are solicited and reviewed.

Based on a five-year review from 1992 to 1997, work RVUs for approximately 300 CPT codes were increased while approximately 120 codes were decreased. Many physician organizations channel their work RVU recommendations through the American Medical Association's Specialty Society RBRVS Update Committee. The purpose of this committee is to allow physician groups to present HCFA with a united front on revisions. Recommendations from specialty societies, commenters, carrier medical directors, and other groups will be considered in the decision process. HCFA has made it clear, however, that its decisions will not be influenced by any particular group.

PRACTICE EXPENSE RVUs

The practice expense portion of RVUs represents the cost to provide patient care. The factor assigned to the practice expense component represents approximately 42 percent of the total RVU.

Practice expense RVUs include both direct costs, such as clinical personnel and medical supplies, and indirect costs, as for office rent and business support.

In 1998 HCFA, due to a mandate in the 1997 Balance Budget Act, began the process of converting from a charge-based to a resource-based practice expense RVU. The conversion (due to be completed by 2001) results in a lowering of practice expense RVUs for all services except those services that are provided at least 75 percent in an office (nonfacility) setting. The practice expense RVUs for services performed in a facility (i.e., hospital, ambulatory surgery center) were likewise reduced.

As a result of the practice expense conversion and the negative impact on specialist reimbursement, a lawsuit was filed by 11 specialty associations in late 1998. The lawsuit alleges that, when fully implemented, the practice expense conversion will result in an overall decline to specialists of approximately $495 million.

When fully implemented, the practice expense RVU will result in an overall increase for services provided in the physician (nonfacility) office. For example, the fully implemented practice expense portion of a mid-level established office visit will be 0.72 as compared with the work RVU component of 0.67 for the same service. Conversely, the practice expense portion of a laparoscopic cholecystectomy (CPT code 56340) is 6.48 as compared to the work RVU of 11.09 for the same service. The practice expense RVU is 107 percent of the work RVU for the office visit and only 58 percent of the work RVU for the surgical procedure.

MALPRACTICE RVUs

The malpractice portion of the RVU represents 3 to 4 percent of the RBRVS payment. The 1997 BBA likewise required that malpractice RVUs be transitioned to a resource-based factor. The malpractice component is calculated based on a weighted average of ratios of malpractice premiums to the revenues of the specialty providing the service. The goal is to produce a national average premium for each specialty.

When fully implemented in 2002, the combined effect of the shift to resource-based practice expense and malpractice expense RVUs will negatively impact certain specialties. This reallocation will result in an increase in office-based RVUs of about 13 percent.

The transition to fully resource-based practice expense RVUs and the resulting shift in practice expenses resulted in a suit filed by 11 medical specialty societies in Chicago U.S. District Court against HCFA. The medical societies contend that HCFA made an error in establishing the base year as 1998 and that, without a correction to the practice expense calculation, they will lose approximately $495 million in reimbursement dollars by the end of the transition.

For example, anesthesiology is projected to experience a 9 percent drop in reimbursement due to the shift in practice expense to office-based services. Other specialties that will be negatively impacted include:

Cardiac surgery	–8%
Thoracic surgery	–6%
Gastroenterology	–4%
Cardiology	–3%
Pulmonary	–2%
General surgery	–1%

Specialties that are projected to benefit from the shift include:

Optometry	+5%
Rheumatology	+4%
General practice	+2%
Podiatry	+2%

GEOGRAPHIC PRACTICE COST INDEX (GPCI)

The geographic practice cost index (GPCI) is a factor assigned to each component in the RBRVS formula to account for cost-of-living disparities in various localities. Only 16 states have more than one locality. The law creating physician payment reform requires HCFA to update GPCIs at least every three years; the last update occurred in 1998.

The geographic cost index includes the following:

- The local opportunity cost of physician time and effort (applied to the work expense portion)
- The local costs of all other expenses of the physician practice (applied to the practice expense portion)
- The local cost of profession liability insurance (applied to the malpractice expense portion)

CONVERSION FACTORS

From 1994 to 1997 three conversion factors existed—one for surgical services, one for nonsurgical services, and one for primary care services. Beginning in 1998, Congress directed HCFA to establish one conversion factor based on a blend of prior years. In 1997 the conversion factor for surgical services was $40.9603; for nonsurgical services, it was $33.8454; and for primary care services, it was $35.7671. In 1998 the blended conversion factor for all services was $36.6873. In 2000 the conversion factor for all services except anesthesia is $36.6137 compared to $34.7315 in 1999. This represents a 5.4 percent increase for year 2000, which is the largest increase since the conversion factor was blended in 1998. The conversion factor for anesthesiology is projected to be $17.77 for 2000 as compared to $17.24 in 1999.

For a compensation system to be based on any relative value scale, the physicians involved must understand the underlying theory behind the scale in order to agree or disagree that those units of measure truly reflect their work ethic. Many consultants will recommend using the work RVU portion only as a basis for allocating income. This concept will be discussed in Chapter 13.

CHAPTER THIRTEEN

Using Relative Value Units to Measure Productivity

The greatest of all gifts is the power to estimate things at their true worth.
—La Rochefoucauld

In the medical practice, productivity may be measured for a variety of reasons. Productivity can be an indicator of general office efficiency. Additionally, productivity may be measured to ensure that there is a reasonable division of work among partners. Productivity is also a primary factor in determining physician compensation. Relative value units (RVUs) can provide a reasonable measurement of work performed in each of these scenarios.

RVUs allow the practice to measure productivity by the work performed, not by the fees generated. Tracking actual work performed also allows the practice to allocate resources properly.

In order to use RVUs to measure productivity, the practice must maintain the appropriate tools. Keep in mind that if something cannot be counted, it cannot be measured. The tools required include:

- A report of production frequency by CPT code. For example, how many times did the physician perform a level III established office visit (CPT code 99213)? If the billing system does not provide a report indicating the frequency of services by provider, it will be difficult to convert to an RBRVS system to measure productivity.

- Current RBRVS listing by CPT code. The current RBRVS values assigned to each CPT code can be found in the *Federal Register*. The final version is generally published annually by October 31.

- Current GPCI (geographic practice cost index). The current geographic adjustment factor is published in the *Federal Register*.
- Financial statements and other financial reporting, if applicable, by physician, department, or location.
- Spreadsheet software to apply RVUs.

Restating productivity in the form of RVUs involves the following five steps:

1. Determine the frequency of each procedure performed during the period being evaluated (month, quarter, semiannual, annual).
2. Determine the components of the RVUs that will be used in the computation. In many cases only the physician work component is used in the conversion process.
3. Apply the GPCI to the RVU.
4. Once the single-scale relative values have been calculated, multiply the frequency of each procedure performed by the corresponding adjusted RVU.
5. Total the RVUs for the period to restate total productivity.

In a simple example, assume Practice A has $450,000 in net income to divide. Charges, collections, and RVUs (work component adjusted for the GPCI) are as follows:

	Charges	Collections	RVUs
Dr. A	$200,000	$140,000	3,800
Dr. B	$300,000	$160,000	5,250
Dr. C	$350,000	$225,000	7,000

Restated as a percentage of the total, the results are as follows:

	Charges	Collections	RVUs
Dr. A	23%	27%	24%
Dr. B	35%	30%	33%
Dr. C	42%	43%	43%

If the practice distributes income based on collections, Dr. B obviously would be underpaid based on work effort. Using RVUs allows the practice to remove the potential problems associated with a disproportionate allocation of poor payors or perhaps a temporary glitch in collections related to services performed.

RVUs also can be used to establish productivity standards to be used in determining minimum standards for base salary amounts. Additionally, the information derived can be used in establishing gross revenues for budgetary purposes.

For instance, assume that the target annual visits for an internal medicine practice are 4,200 visits, which equates to 2,800 RVUs. Actual results for the compensation period are as follows:

	Actual Visits	**RVUs**
Dr. A	4,700	2,810
Dr. B	4,300	3,064

The percentage of actual in excess of the standard (4,200 visits, 2,800 RVUs) is as follows:

	% of Visits	**% of RVUs**
Dr. A	11.90%	.35%
Dr. B	2.38%	9.42%

As discussed in previous chapters, the compensation system should not provide incentives for upcoding. In this scenario, compensation based totally on RVUs could reward Dr. B for aggressive coding, certainly not a wise practice.

Therefore, a weighting of the two standards may be appropriate. If the standards are given equal weight (50 percent to each), the following results are achieved:

	Weighted % of Standard
Dr. A	6.13%
Dr. B	5.90%

By using a weighted percentage, the practice has compensated Dr. A for visits in excess of standard while taking into consideration that Dr. B may be treating more complicated patients.

RVUs IN CAPITATION

The use of RVUs to measure productivity also works well in a capitated environment. In a capitated plan, the practice receives a per member per month amount regardless of the number of patients that are treated. Using a fee-for-service equivalent charge to measure productivity may not accurately reflect the services provided by a physician.

Capitation transfers much of the financial risk from the payor to the provider through the fixed per member per month reimbursement. Therefore, the obvious way to increase income is through cost controls. RVUs make the appropriate allocation of practice overhead easier to obtain. Care, however, must be exercised in determining which costs to match with which RVUs. To do this, a practice manager must prepare the organization's financial statements on a departmental basis. Income statements identifying revenue centers with the appropriate direct costs (labor, medical supplies, etc.) and the appropriate allocated indirect costs (phone, utilities, administration, etc.) must be established. The recommended approach is to review line items in the existing chart of accounts and allocate each line item to a specific revenue center. Those expenses that cannot be assigned directly must be allocated on a basis agreed to by all of the physicians. This allocation of overhead to the appropriate departments is crucial to the process of arriving at accurate information that provides management with an effective decision-making tool.

COSTS PER RVU

The next step in determining costs per service or by physician is to develop cost per RVU. Two steps are involved in developing costs per RVU for revenue centers:

1. Total the number of RVUs generated by the CPT codes classified to each revenue center.
2. Divide the total costs allocated to each revenue center by the total number of RVUs generated by that center.

The result is the cost per RVU for the services in that revenue center. Cost per RVU is a vital piece of information when determining the overall profitability of a practice. This information is also useful when negotiating fee schedules and contracts.

Keep in mind that, in all scenarios, designated health services must be divided regardless of the services ordered by individual physicians. In the preceding examples, it is assumed that designated health services have been carved out of the compensation formula prior to the allocation by RVUs.

CHAPTER FOURTEEN

Cost Allocation

In the design of compensation systems, much time and effort is directed toward the allocation of revenue. Revenue may be assigned based on charge volume or collections or restated in the form of relative value units (RVUs). Obviously a proper allocation of revenue is essential for a sound compensation model. However, attention likewise must be directed toward the division of expenses (overhead).

With managed care and government programs (Medicare and Medicaid) controlling 74 percent of group practice revenue through capitation and/or discounted fee-for-service revenues, monitoring overhead is essential to maintain profitability. Accurate expense identification and allocation is likewise essential for a sound compensation formula.

In the past, most practices allocated costs based on revenue, whether charges or collections define revenue. For instance, an allocation of net income based on a production percentage defined as charges assumes that all costs are variable and increase proportionately with increases in revenue. The same would be true using any measure of production as the basis for allocating costs.

In multispecialty practices, the variable allocation of practice costs can cause disproportionate expense assignment in the compensation model. For example, assume a pediatrician and a surgeon share office space. The pediatrician has office hours for four and one-half days per week and uses four exam rooms. The surgeon, on the other hand, uses two exam rooms and has office hours three days per week. A variable sharing of practice costs could result in the following disproportionate allocation:

Monthly Practice Expenses

Rent	$5,000
Administrative salaries and benefits	7,100
Clinical salaries and benefits	3,750

Medical supplies	1,100	
Other	16,000	
Total	$32,950	

Monthly Practice Collections

Pediatrician	$32,000	(44%)
Surgeon	41,000	(56%)
Total	$73,000	

Expenses Allocated by Collections

Pediatrician	($32,950 × 44%)	$14,500
Surgeon	($32,950 × 56%)	18,450

In this example, each physician is allocated expenses at the same percentage of collections (45 percent). However, the surgeon, who uses less of the practice resources, is saddled with 27 percent more overhead dollars than the pediatrician. The pediatrician is obviously benefiting from economies of scale since the median overhead percentage for pediatricians based on the Medical Group Management Association (MGMA) 1999 Report is 54.88 percent of collections. The surgeon, on the other hand, is penalized in this allocation with a 45 percent overhead amount. The median overhead percentage for general surgeons in the MGMA survey is 37.88 percent.

The preceding example points out the discrepancies that can occur if practice costs are allocated based only on production. Should a physician be penalized for generating a higher level of income based on charges, collections, or RVUs? Shouldn't there be some consideration for utilization of practice resources?

In order to resolve these inaccuracies, a careful allocation of practice costs must occur. Practice expenses should be allocated based on the following categories:

- Direct
- Equal
- Utilization
- Volume

DIRECT EXPENSES

Direct expenses constitute those costs that are directly assignable to, and to some degree may be controllable by, the physician. Costs in this category may include continuing medical education (CME), dues and subscriptions, cellular phones, malpractice insurance, fringe benefit costs (health, life, and disability insurance), and qualified plan contributions.

In some cases practices will establish a limit or allowance on certain direct expenses, such as cellular phones and CME. Obviously some limits must be placed on these expense items, otherwise physicians may incur costs in excess of what is financially feasible for the practice. Consideration should be given as to whether these expense items will be considered operational expenses in determining net income before physician compensation or as a component of the physician compensation pool.

Other direct expenses may include the cost for a clinical employee (i.e., registered nurse, medical assistant) directly assigned to the physician. Another example would be for practices in which each physician employs a secretary; the related salary and benefit expense may be allocated directly to the physician.

Costs of furnishing an office may be a direct allocation to the physician. Furnishings and computers should be governed by a set dollar limitation and by frequency of purchase. Most office furnishings should have a 5-to 10-year life, with computers being replaced every three years.

EQUAL EXPENSES

Certain practice costs do not fluctuate based on utilization or volume of services provided. These expense items may exist regardless of the number of patient encounters or the charges generated by the practice. Items that may be divided equally among the providers in the practice might include legal and accounting expenses, telephone, practice manager/administrator's salary and benefits, and advertising/promotional expenses.

If the practice is single specialty or multispecialty with similar office hours, it may be practical to divide all administrative salaries and benefits equally, as well as rent expense. If, however, the physicians maintain significantly different schedules and office utilization (as in the example of the pediatrician and the surgeon), administrative salaries and rent may be allocated more appropriately by utilization. A careful analysis of utilization is required. Although the physician may not be in the office suite full time, he or she most likely will require office space on a full-time basis. Therefore, rent may contain both a fixed and a variable component. Rent should be allocated to any Stark (ancillary) revenue centers to determine net ancillary income.

For instance, if one physician uses four exam rooms and another uses two exam rooms, perhaps rent should be allocated two-thirds/one-third respectively. Along the same line, if one physician maintains a four-day office schedule and another maintains a two-day schedule, perhaps the receptionist's salary and other related front office expenses should be allocated similarly (two-thirds/one-third).

Most likely the billing staff salary and benefits should be divided equally. In our example with the pediatrician and the surgeon, if the billing office salaries were allocated based on volume, the surgeon would pay the greater expense with an obviously lower volume of actual transactions. However, the surgeon's billing might entail more coding expertise and follow-up time. If the billing office is allocated on any basis besides equal, the practice may, once again, be "splitting hairs".

UTILIZATION

In multispecialty practices, certain expenses should be allocated based on utilization. An equal allocation in cases of significant disproportionate use can result in an inappropriate division of practice costs. For instance, rent and certain clinical and administrative salaries may be allocated based on utilization.

Careful consideration, however, must be given to multioffice, multispecialty practices. Assume, for instance, that a practice decides to open an office in a typically retail center (i.e., shopping mall) for exposure and/or a walk-in clinic. The rent in this location may exceed that of other locations for the practice. If costs are allocated specifically to a site, the physicians at the higher-cost site may be unduly penalized. In most multioffice situations, the best alternative would be to pool all costs and then assign the pooled costs based on individual utilization.

For example, if Physician A requires the use of three exam rooms of the 27 total exam rooms maintained by the practice, he or she would be allocated one-ninth (11 percent) of the pooled space cost. In the cases of multilocation practices that maintain a central administrative/billing location, it may be advisable to divide the cost of the central office equally among the providers.

VOLUME

Certain expenses will vary directly with volume (volume being defined as charges, collections, RVUs, patient visits, number of surgeries, etc.). The most obvious variable expense is medical supplies. Other variable expenses may include laboratory expense and radiology (X-ray) expense. Lab and radiology are designated health services, therefore, costs associated with those services should be allocated to the Stark revenue center.

Variable expenses should be allocated based on volume and/or production. Once again, to determine if the basis for allocation of costs is reasonable and fair, we must define production. In the allocation of variable costs, production may be defined as:

- Gross charges
- Collections
- RVUs
- Number of patient visits
- Number of hours worked
- New patient visits
- Number of surgical cases
- Number of employees
- Or any other basis that is determined to be reasonable and fair

The underlying theory should be a determination of cause and effect. What activity fluctuations (cause) affects an expense to the extent it will increase or decrease based on those fluctuations?

A careful allocation of practice costs is essential in establishing an equitable compensation model. However, allocating each expense item differently on a monthly or quarterly basis may become cumbersome. Direct expenses should be maintained separately so that they can be allocated directly with each distribution. The more direct expenses that are identified, the more accurate the allocation.

PRIOR YEAR ALLOCATION METHOD

The above discussions represent an allocation of costs based on actual performance during a period. Expenses also may be allocated based on a prior year's performance and adjusted on a periodic basis during the current year to reflect variances. For example, assume that a cost analysis of the practice for the prior year indicated that one-third of total practice costs should be allocated equally and two-thirds should be divided based on production. These amounts could be used throughout the year and adjusted based on actual costs at year-end. Another example would be to develop a cost conversion factor per RVU based on historical data with quarterly, semiannual, or annual revisions.

EXHIBIT 14.1
Allocation of Overhead Based on RVUs

Analysis of Cost per RVU (Expense Conversion Factor)

Total operating expenses (overhead) year ended 12/31/xx	$2,120,000
Total RVUs generated for year ended 12/31/xx	#125,000
Cost per RVU (expense conversion factor)	$16.96

Cost Allocation

Physician	RVUs year ended 12/31/xx	Overhead × $16.96
Dr. A	30,000	$508,800
Dr. B	60,000	$1,017,600
Dr. C	45,000	$763,200

Exhibit 14.1 presents an example of costs allocated based on RVUs. The practice, in the example, allocates practice overhead based on the number of RVUs generated by each physician.

Total costs then would be allocated on a monthly basis to each physician based on his or her actual RVU production from the prior month. This method assumes that expenses paid in the current month are related to the services provided in the prior month. An analysis may be performed quarterly to determine if the overhead conversion factor has increased or decreased materially, which would result in a revision for the upcoming quarter.

Obviously these calculations can be determined at various levels of reporting. It may be appropriate for the group to segregate costs to revenue centers and then to physicians within that revenue center. It should be a determination of what is fair in deciding the appropriate allocation method.

In multispecialty practices that include both primary care and specialty physicians, most specialists accept the fact that their overhead percentage may be higher than single-specialty practices. The offsetting benefit should be the advantage of captive "gatekeepers" who provide referrals to the specialists within the multispecialty group. The specialists will pay an overhead "tax" for the benefit of association with primary care "gatekeepers."

If the above allocation (equal, utilization, variable) were applied to our original example (pediatrician and surgeon), the following result could be obtained:

	Pediatrician	**Surgeon**
Rent (2/3, 1/3)	$3,300	$1,700
Administrative salaries (1/2, 1/2)	3,550	3,550
Clinical salaries (2/3, 1/3)	2,500	1,250
Medical supplies (volume)	700	400
Other (revenue)	7,000	9,000
Total	$17,050	$15,900
Collections	$32,000	$41,000
Overhead as a % of collections	53.3%	38.8%

The more specific allocation of expenses in this example has resulted in an overhead allocation that is comparable to the MGMA survey median (54.88 percent for pediatric, 37.88 percent for surgery) compared to the previous 45 percent overhead allocation to each physician based on a percent of collection allocation across the board.

STARK REVENUES

Assigning costs appropriately is important in the allocation of Stark revenues. Stark I and Stark II laws require physicians to allocate income derived from designated health services on a basis other than direct referral. The basis for allocation cannot include the value or volume of the referrals for these services. In other words, physicians cannot include gross charges, collections, or number of visits or patients from designated health services they have ordered in their direct revenue for income distribution purposes. Designated health services include:

- Clinical laboratory services
- Physical therapy services
- Occupational therapy services
- Radiology services, including magnetic resonance imaging (MRI), computerized axial tomography (CAT) scans, and ultrasound services
- Radiation therapy services and supplies
- Durable medical equipment and supplies
- Parenteral and enteral nutrients, equipment, and supplies
- Prosthetics, orthotics, and prosthetic devices and supplies
- Home health services

- Outpatient prescription drugs
- Inpatient and outpatient hospital services

All costs (direct and indirect) related to the provision of designated health services should be allocated to the designated health service income before the revenue is divided. This piece of the pie should be defined as net Stark revenue. Specific cost allocation can assist in easing the effect of reallocating Stark revenues in a group practice.

All direct costs incurred in the provision of designated health service revenue should be assigned to either a single Stark revenue center or to individual Stark service centers. Direct costs include salaries and benefits of clinical personnel (i.e., registered nurses, laboratory and radiology technologists, physical therapists), supplies, depreciation expenses related to designated health service equipment, allocated rent, and license fees. Indirect costs include an allocation for general and administrative expenses. Indirect costs may be allocated to designated health services based on a percentage of designated health service revenue (charges or collections) to total revenue (charges or collections). As many of the Stark services do not have corresponding RVUs, using RVUs would not be an appropriate method of allocating costs.

CHAPTER FIFTEEN

Administering the Compensation Plan

*A committee is a cul-de-sac down which
ideas are lured and then quietly strangled.*
—Sir Barnett Cocks

The success of a well-designed physician compensation plan is contingent on the ability of the group to administer and monitor the plan. Trust and respect must exist between physicians and the practice. Physicians must understand and accept the compensation plan. In order for the plan to be effective, the physician must clearly understand how his or her behavior will influence compensation. Incentives established in the plan should result in the desired behavior which supports and promotes group goals.

In order to administer a compensation plan effectively, the group must have stable, effective leadership. The leadership group must include physician leaders who understand and promote the group goals. If the practice is administered solely by nonphysician leaders, failure is likely. The group must have strong physician leaders who are able to lead and to encourage their physician peers.

One of the greatest changes in the role of the senior physician executives in today's healthcare provider organizations is the way in which they view themselves. In the early 1990s a national survey reported that 80 percent of physicians thought of themselves as clinicians, 13 percent as leaders, and 6 percent as managers. A similar survey conducted five years later revealed that 47 percent view themselves as leaders, 42 percent as physicians, and 10 percent as managers. Such a transformation in perception in so short a time is remarkable.

The changes run deep. Most of today's physician executives have acquired substantial management training and experience, and many have worked with and depended on the experience and expertise of physician executive mentors for their career guidance and development.

> *Leaders are best when people barely know they exist, not so good*
> *when people obey and acclaim them, worse when people*
> *despise them. But of good leaders, who talk little, when their work is*
> *finished, their aim fulfilled, the others will say, "We did it ourselves."*
>
> —Lao Tzu

The movement away from authoritarian leadership and toward team development began over 2,000 years ago, as evidenced by the above observation of Lao Tzu, a Chinese philosopher. Today's organizations are continuing to develop leadership that empowers rather than overpowers.

There is no standard "test" for leadership. Physicians considering a leadership role should consider the following questions:

- Am I excited about the prospect of being a successful leader?
- Do I feel that I am ready to accept this responsibility?
- Do I have a vision of where I think the organization should be (long term and short term)?
- Do I feel that the group will support me in a leadership role?

Successful physician leaders should possess the following characteristics:

- Clarity of purpose: Physician leaders should consider their motives carefully. The desire to lead should come from a commitment and drive to make positive change in the group practice, not from a personal desire to control or exert personal influence. Clarity of mission and dedication to the goals and objectives of the group are essential qualities for successful physician leaders.
- Ability to motivate others toward the group vision: Vision is the ability to imagine and communicate a different, improved future and then motivate followers to get there. A leader's vision gives an organization the ability to see itself crossing the goal line while still struggling up the field. Vision is the ability to maneuver around obstacles while still moving forward.

  Physician leaders must be able to articulate the group vision for the future and help others understand and work toward attaining it.

Often this requires aligning individual goals with the needs of the organization to gain commitment. The effective physician leader must be able to assist the group in creating a vision and then must enable the group to achieve the vision by removing obstacles and sharing information freely.

- Ability to build trust and credibility: Personal credibility is the single most important element of leadership. A major role of leaders in the future will be to take organizations through dramatic, fast-paced change.

  The successful physician leader must be trusted by those he or she leads. Success in clinical practice and understanding of clinical issues are essential in building credibility. Personal integrity and honesty are characteristics that contribute to the establishment of trust.

- Persistence when faced with obstacles: The physician who gives up too soon when obstacles arise often fails. The drive to persist comes from a strong commitment to the group's vision and goals.

- Organizational savvy: The effective leader must be able to develop a strong base of influence within the organization as well as within the community. Success depends on the physician leader's ability to build consensus within the organization. Building consensus requires high skill levels in negotiation and persuasion.

  Admired leaders are those who are able to create and maintain organizational balance. They know that teamwork and empowerment are not inconsistent with the demands of organizational structure.

  Effective leaders must be able to let go. Leaders must be able to do more than delegate. They must be able to inspire those they lead through the establishment of goals, outcomes, accountability, responsibility, authority, and results.

- Exhibit an attitude of service: Leaders must truly care about their followers. Autocratic, controlling behavior is not a desired attribute for an effective leader. The effective leader must possess the skills of listening, inspiring, coaching, delegating, and guiding. A high regard for diversity of opinions must be evident. Arrogant, ego-involved, self-centered leaders will certainly fail. As soon as a leader begins to feel that it is lonely at the top, he or she probably is not spending enough time observing and communicating. A leader who feels isolated probably is. Compassionate leaders communicate effectively. Leadership is a role that requires humility and a high regard for the needs of others.

- Ability to give praise and recognition: Leaders who are able to provide praise and recognition are more likely to maintain a high level of enthusiasm and commitment.

- Self-awareness: Effective physician leaders must recognize their own personal strengths and weaknesses. They must pursue self-knowledge and improvement continually.

The organizational structure must provide for physician involvement with clear lines of authority and decision making. The board members, president, and medical director must be absolutely trustworthy. They must commit to working for the best interests of the group and avoid conflicts of interest.

The physician group should elect a centralized management group (board of directors, executive committee) to manage the operational aspects of the group based on predetermined goals and strategies. The central management group should have the ability to formulate strategy and develop policy. For example, the board of directors may approve the annual budget. The central management group should be responsible for developing strategy (perhaps with the input of a finance committee in larger practices) to administer the budget. The central management team should be accountable to the practice for its actions and should have the respect and authority to lead.

If additional management committees are established (i.e., finance, public relations, recruiting/retention, quality improvement), the purpose for the committee should be clearly defined along with its lines of authority and decision-making capacity. A well-designed committee structure can provide for efficient management. However, if the committees are ill informed and act independently, their effectiveness will be minimal. Furthermore, the success of the group may be impeded if decisions are made that run counter to group goals and strategies.

The medical director plays an important leadership role. He or she is a physician leader who is charged with the responsibility of managing the conduct of the physician group in accordance with group policies and objectives. A physician governance or professional practice committee can be formed to assist the medical director in carrying out his or her duties. The committee can provide a forum for physician comments and concerns. Additionally, the committee can assist in the evaluation process for physician performance.

Likewise, the group must maintain a strong management infrastructure. Practices with a strong, effective infrastructure will command the respect of the physicians within the group. Especially in the case of merging practices, a centralized management system is essential. Diverse management in a group practice is a recipe for disaster.

The group must maintain the policies and procedures necessary to support sound management principles. Practice failures typically occur due to inefficient management. If the practice is not managed properly, billing and collections may suffer and expenses may not be managed appropriately. The result is a declining bottom line that results in declining income for the physician group. Declining physician income typically leads to friction within the group and division.

The practice must maintain an efficient evaluation system for physicians. Physicians must be advised in a timely manner where they stand on meeting objectives. For instance, if physicians are to be evaluated on a certain number of patient visits as a base criteria, the practice should provide a periodic report (preferably monthly) to provide physicians with appropriate data so that they can adjust behavior to meet the specified goals.

The evaluation process should provide an opportunity to establish objective and constructive dialog between the physician and the practice. In large practices, the medical director may be delegated to perform physician evaluations. Questionnaires and patient surveys may be used as part of the evaluation process.

Physicians traditionally have preferred the utilization of a performance checklist. The checklist may set forth the predetermined evaluation parameters compared with actual results. Periodic evaluations are advisable, especially when corrective action is needed. It is unfair to inform a physician after the fact that performance goals have not been met. The physician should be counseled during the year so he or she may take corrective action.

The financial condition of the practice should be reported to the physician group in a timely manner. A fundamental objective of all compensation plans is to maintain the financial viability of the practice. In order for the compensation plan to be effective, physicians must understand and trust the financial information provided. Likewise, they must understand how their behavior impacts the financial results of the practice.

The compensation system must be managed and administered efficiently. The reporting format for computations must be in understandable, reliable format. If physicians doubt the reliability of the computations, they will doubt the soundness of the formula on which they are based. Sample formula computations can be prepared periodically during the computation period. For instance, a semiannual computation might be prepared for an annual incentive bonus. There should be no surprises. The physician group should be informed (good or bad) as to the direction of the bonus calculation.

CHAPTER SIXTEEN

Academic Group Practice Compensation Models

The classic financial model indicates that return increases proportionately with risk. In the past, this was certainly true in the traditional group medical practice. Physicians who chose the entrepreneurial route traded long hours and the associated risk for higher income. Academic practice provided a more secure environment with decreased administrative burdens and reduced risk. The trade-off for physicians was less compensation than entrepreneurial counterparts received.

With the increase of managed care, physicians are faced with greater administrative burdens, increased expenses, and lower reimbursement. Independent group practice physicians are consequently rethinking the risk/return ratio. As one physician expressed the dilemma, "My crap-to-joy ratio in private practice is out of sync."

Academic practice provides physicians with a secure environment along with the opportunity to pursue teaching and research activities. Medical schools, however, are faced with the same negative impact from managed care as private practice. Declines in reimbursement have caused the percentage of clinical salaries to increase from 30 percent to 46 percent of revenue.

Three factors complicate the design of compensation systems for physicians in the academic arena:

1. Compensation, in many cases, may already be below market based on the specialty. In other words, the academic physician has already sacrificed income for security and environment.

2. Academic formulas must consider additional factors not present in private practice formulas (i.e., research grant responsibilities, teaching activities).
3. The pie is shrinking.

Typically, academic practice physicians receive a guaranteed base salary from the medical school along with an incentive payment provided by academic practice clinical income. The medical school salary compensates academic physicians for teaching and research duties. The incentive piece is variable based on the physicians' net share of clinical income and compensates them for clinical productivity.

Since most academic medical centers are not for profit, adherence to specific regulations pertaining to the sharing of revenues is critical. Noncompliance with government regulations could cause the facility to lose its not-for-profit status.

Certain parameters must be considered in designing an academic compensation model:

- The organization must have established goals and the compensation system must offer incentives for the activities that will allow the entity to achieve its mission.
- The academic entity must maintain a system that provides equitable compensation for teaching and research functions.
- The plan must support and provide for the financial security of the facility. Physicians must not be compensated in a fashion that would put the entity at financial risk. The plan must offer incentives for productivity, the proper use of resources, and cost controls.
- The formula must be understandable and perceived as fair by physicians.
- Physicians' interests must be aligned with the goals and mission of the facility.
- The plan must be competitive in the marketplace. It must provide for a level of compensation that will allow the facility to attract quality physicians.

Within the parameters of the compensation plan, the facility must adhere strictly to regulations promulgated by agencies such as the Department of Health and Human Services (DHHS), the National Institutes of Health (NIH), the Health Care Financing Administration (HCFA), and the Internal Revenue Service.

The National Institutes of Health regulates many of the research and training programs that are supported by the federal government. In certain circumstances the NIH will establish maximum salaries that can be paid for services within a grant program.

Teaching hospitals have undergone significant investigations and scrutiny from the Department of Health and Human Services and the Department of Justice regarding billing policies for the services of resident physicians. Investigations into billing practices resulted in a $30 million settlement at one institution and a $12 million settlement at another. The settlements resulted from the government's position that claims were filed on behalf of faculty physicians for services performed by residents without documentation of the involvement of the attending physician. Additionally, the government took the position that claims for certain services were upcoded.

Physicians in teaching hospitals (and in skilled nursing facilities with teaching programs) may be paid under the RBRVS fee schedule just like any other physicians. Teaching physicians can either bill Medicare directly or establish an arrangement for the hospital to bill Part B for their services.

Medicare reimburses the teaching hospital directly instead of the physician in two cases:

1. The teaching hospital is reimbursed directly when it elects to receive payment on a reasonable-cost basis for the direct medical and surgical services of its physicians. In this scenario, all physicians who furnish Medicare-covered services in the facility agree not to bill independently for those services.

2. Payment will be made directly to the teaching hospital on a cost basis if all the physicians are employees of the hospital and are precluded from billing Medicare for these services as a condition of employment.

Teaching physicians who bill Medicare are paid as attending physicians even when interns and residents actually provide the care, as long as physicians direct the interns/residents and the type and quality of care are equal to the care that physicians would give their own patients. Teaching physicians may bill for residents' services only if residents meet Medicare's definition of a resident and are not medical students. A medical student is never considered to be a resident. Any contribution of a medical student to the performance of a service or a billable procedure (with the exception of taking a history in the case of an evaluation and management [E & M] service) must performed in the physical presence of a physician.

Teaching physicians do not have to be physically present during key portions of E & M services that are low- and mid-level codes for office or other outpatient services for either new or established patients. Carriers may provide Medicare physician fee schedule payments to teaching physicians for services furnished by residents without the presence of the teaching physician if all of the following conditions are met:

- Services must be furnished in a family practice center or other center located in an outpatient department of a hospital or another ambulatory care entity in which the time spent by residents in patient care activities is included in determining intermediary (Part A) payments to the hospital.

- Residents furnishing the services without the presence of a teaching physician must have completed more than six months of an approved residency program.

- The teaching physician must not direct the care of more than four residents at any given time and must be immediately available. The teaching physician must have no other responsibilities at the time of the service for which payment is sought. Additionally, he or she must assume management responsibilities for the patients treated by the residents. The teaching physician must ensure that the services provided are appropriate and review with each resident the medical history, physical examination, diagnosis, and records of tests and therapies before or immediately after each visit. Documentation as to the extent of the teaching physician's participation in the review and direction of the services provided must be included in the patient's medical record.

  If one (or more) of the four residents supervised by the teaching physician is still in his or her first six months of training, then the teaching physician must be physically present for the key portion of the encounter between the patient and the resident.

- Residents may furnish the following services in the facility: acute care for undifferentiated problems or chronic care for ongoing conditions; coordination of care furnished by other physicians or providers; comprehensive care not limited by organ system, diagnosis, or sex.

- Patients treated in the teaching facility must consider the facility to be their continuing source of healthcare.

A teaching hospital may elect to receive payment on a reasonable-cost basis for the direct medical and surgical services of its physicians in lieu of fee schedule payments for such services. A teaching hospital may make this election to receive cost payment only when all physicians who render covered Medicare services in the hospital agree in writing not to bill charges for such services. Additionally, the hospital may receive payments when all physicians are employees of the hospital and, as a condition of their employment, are precluded from billing for such services. When the election is made, Medicare payments are made exclusively by the hospital's intermediary, and fee schedule payment is precluded.

When the cost election is made for a current or future period, each physician who provides services to Medicare beneficiaries must agree in writing (except when the employment restriction just discussed exists) not to bill charges for services provided to Medicare beneficiaries. However, when each physician agrees in writing to abide by all the rules and regulations of the medical staff of the hospital, such an agreement suffices if required as a condition of staff privileges and if the rules and regulations of the hospital, medical staff, or fund clearly preclude physician billing for the services for which benefits are payable. The intermediary must advise the carrier when a hospital elects cost payment for physicians' direct medical and surgical services and supply the carrier with a list of all physicians who provide services in the facility.

Medicare reimbursement and the resulting investigations have impacted compensation for physician services in teaching hospitals. As enforcement proceedings continue, the facilities may be negatively impacted financially, thus affecting physician compensation.

The Internal Revenue Service plays a significant role in the monitoring of physician compensation in not-for-profit academic facilities. The IRS maintains that a tax-exempt entity must comply with the Medicare fraud and abuse laws to maintain its status as a 501(c)(3) tax-exempt entity. Paying or receiving compensation for referral of patients is considered a criminal offense. Any incentive or salary component that rewards the physician for referrals is illegal.

Additionally, the tax code provides that a 501(c)(3) organization must function for charitable and/or education purposes. The entity is precluded from allowing surplus earnings to inure to the benefit of private individuals. Consequently, teaching hospitals must exercise extreme care when structuring physician compensation plans. Compensation cannot be in excess of the fair market value for the services rendered. Care must taken in the establishment of incentive plans so that physicians are reasonably compensated for services not an inurement of surplus.

Compensating physicians in the academic setting includes the same challenges as private practice (maintaining productivity, controlling costs, aligning incentives, maintaining quality) as well as additional challenges provided by teaching and research activities. Academic compensation models must provide competitive compensation based on the specialty and service performed. Likewise, strict adherence to government regulations must be maintained.

The most common academic model provides a guaranteed salary for teaching and research services and an incentive based on clinical services provided. The incentive piece should consider quality and patient satisfaction issues in addition to productivity. Typically, collections for professional services (in compliance with Stark regulations) are included in the physician incentive less applicable direct and indirect overhead. Typically, indirect overhead includes an allocation of administrative expense incurred by the academic entity. From physicians' perspectives, the administrative allocation may appear arbitrary and be viewed as an academic "tax" incurred by physicians for the benefit of providing services in the academic setting.

CHAPTER SEVENTEEN

Physician Integration Systems

He who dies with the most PCPs wins.
—Unknown

Fueled by the restrictions imposed by managed care, hospitals have sought to form alliances with physicians. In the earliest stages, physicians and hospitals formed alliances through physician-hospital organizations (PHOs). PHOs often have as their principle focus the organization of physicians into a physician-contracting relationship. A joint governing board comprised of physician and hospital representation is established to provide a vehicle for joint decision making. The PHO provides a coordinated approach to managed care contracting by creating and coordinating contracting networks consisting of the physician practices and the hospital.

The PHO model is integration in its simplest form. It requires the practice and the hospital to negotiate and cooperate for managed care contracting purposes. Physicians remain employed by their independent practices and maintain their respective salaries and benefit plans. The only impact on the practice occurs based on the managed care reimbursement negotiated by the PHO. Otherwise, the hospital and the practices operate separately.

Beyond the PHO, hospitals have formed management alliances with practice groups and, in the strongest sense of alliance, have acquired practices and employed physicians. Acquisitions of practices provide the hospital with ambulatory care options that enable it to extend services beyond inpatient care.

Medical groups considering acquisition and employment by hospitals are faced with a difficult decision. The greatest barrier to integration is typically a fear of loss of independence. However, that fear may be outweighed by the following perceived benefits:

- Groups may be attracted by the capital and resources that the hospital is able to offer. Tax laws encourage practices to empty the coffers at year end, leaving no resources or capital for expansion.
- Many physicians are simply weary of the administrative burden of private practice. They envision the hospital alliance as a means to rid themselves of the day-to-day grind of practice management. The hospital appears to be a sophisticated source of practice management resources.
- Practices experiencing rising expenses may perceive a hospital alliance as a means to control overhead costs.
- Increased managed care pressures may cause practices to become concerned about the effect of competition. The hospital alliance may be viewed as a means to obtain security in managed care contracting.

Physician-hospital integration can occur through three basic types of entities:

1. The management services organization model
2. The foundation model
3. The hospital-owned physician practice model

MANAGEMENT SERVICES ORGANIZATION MODEL

The Management Services Organization Model (MSO) is the least integrated of the physician-hospital integration options. The MSO is a separate entity that is formed to provide comprehensive management services to the medical practice. MSOs generally provide at least the services of PHO, including managed care contracting, UR, and QA, to the extent permissible by law and regulation.

The MSO should be a real business, not a sham, and it should be sufficiently capitalized consistent with a business plan. It should have a true business purpose and demonstrate the attributes of an ordinary business entity. Goods and services must be provided for a reasonable fee, and there can be no payments for the referral of patients.

Typically, the MSO will purchase the business assets of the practice (i.e., office space, equipment, furnishings, billing system) and hire the business office employees; however, the practice maintains its separate identity. The medical group continues to own its medical records, employ and supervise its clinical staff, and collect fees for services rendered.

The MSO is not a "provider" or "supplier" of physician or hospital services. Goods and services are provided to the physician practices, not to the patients. The consequences of the MSO assuming the provider role may constitute unauthorized practice of medicine and violation of corporate practice of medicine doctrine or medical practices acts.

The MSO may act as the agent of the physician or physician group for billing. Although Medicare regulations prohibit the assignment of claims by providers, Medicare may pay an agent who furnishes billing and collection services to a provider if the following conditions are met:

- The agent receives the payment under an agency agreement with the provider.
- The agent's compensation is not related in any way to the dollar amounts billed or collected.
- The agent's compensation is not dependent on the actual collection of payment.
- The agent acts under payment disposition instructions that the provider may modify or revoke at any time.
- The agent, in receiving the payment, acts only on behalf of the provider.
- Payment to an agent will always be made in the name of the provider.

MSOs are subject to the Medicare fraud and abuse and antikickback laws. No Medicare payments can be made to an MSO because the MSO is not a provider. Activities of MSOs that are controlled by a hospital may be attributed to the hospital for purposes of analysis under antikickback laws.

Each of the three services provided by the MSO must be analyzed under the applicable Medicare safe harbor regulations:

1. Space lease
   - The agreement must be in writing and signed.
   - The agreement must specify the premises covered by the lease.
   - The agreement must specify periodic intervals, if applicable.
   - The term of the agreement must be not less than one year in duration.
   - The rent charged must be set in advance at fair market value and not be related to the volume or value of referrals.

2. Equipment lease
   - The agreement must be in writing and signed.
   - The agreement must specify the equipment covered by the lease.
   - The agreement must specify periodic intervals, if applicable.
   - The term of the agreement must be not less than one year in duration.
   - The rental fee must fall within a reasonable commercial range.
3. Personal services/management contract
   - The agreement must be in writing and signed.
   - The agreement must specify the services to be performed.
   - The agreement must specify periodic intervals, if applicable.
   - The term of the agreement must be not less than one year in duration.
   - The fee charged must be within a reasonable commercial range based on fair market value.
   - The services performed cannot be in violation of federal or state law.
   - The parties should keep meticulous records of services provided.

The MSO structure allows the practice to contract with the hospital for management services while maintaining its organizational independence. As such, the practice maintains full operational risk. The MSO model does not provide security for physician income.

FOUNDATION MODEL

A medical foundation is a nonprofit organization employing or contracting with physicians and/or physician groups to provide medical services. The foundation model provides the physician and hospital with an intermediate form of integration.

The foundation is established as a separate entity and becomes the provider of care. As the provider of care, the foundation arranges for care, maintains the patient relationship, and employs the clinical personnel (exclusive of the physicians) necessary to deliver care.

Its activities might include:

- The operation of outpatient clinics in facilities that it owns or leases

does not necessarily include a payment component, such as an HMO, although it may.

Under this model, physicians become employees of the hospital or its subsidiary. In many cases, a hospital may acquire an existing practice and subsequently employ its physicians. As such, the physicians are completely integrated in the overall delivery system.

The model may be established in one of four ways:

1. Single organization—owns and operates the hospital

   - Employs physicians. Once established, the integrated delivery system structure has little risk from Medicare fraud and abuse and Stark perspective because all elements are part of one corporation and the physicians are employees. Thus, the safe harbor for employees is met. However, Part B billing issues may arise due to integration.

   - Contracts with physicians as independent contractors. The risk of Medicare fraud and abuse and Stark violations is greater with this structure since the physicians are not employees. The Part B billing issues must be closely scrutinized in this form of consolidation.

2. Parent holding company model

   - Parent holding company is the sole member of a nonprofit hospital or the shareholder of investor-owned hospitals.

   - Parent holding company is the sole member of a nonprofit medical foundation, which either employs or contracts with physicians or the shareholder of the investor-owned medical group. The parties should ensure compliance with group practice or the employment exception to Stark II.

   - Possible future wholly owned subsidiary safe harbor to the fraud and abuse laws that might offer protection seems to be less of a possibility today.

   - The Part B issues, once again, are important in this form of consolidation.

3. Physician-controlled system

   - Physicians or physician group owns a hospital.

   - Less risk from a Medicare fraud and abuse and Stark perspective because of structure.

   - Medicare Part B issues may arise as part of the consolidation.

4. Hospital-controlled system
   - Hospital is the sole member of a nonprofit foundation that employs or contracts with physicians or the shareholder of the investor-owned medical group.
   - Risks are similar to the parent holding company model.
   - Medicare Part B issues may arise as part of the consolidation.

An important component of the integrated delivery system is physician compensation and how to offer incentives to physicians. The Stark regulations impact the methodology used in the division of income in the same way that they impact group practice formulas and medical foundation model formulas. However, hospital owners of group medical practices have realized the impact of not providing proper incentives to physician owners. In many cases, physicians reduce productivity after acquisition, thus negatively impacting the organization's financial viability.

The Internal Revenue Service carefully scrutinizes audit compensation paid by exempt organizations. Physician and healthcare executive compensation paid by exempt organizations is under scrutiny because:

- It impacts health care costs.
- It raises legal issues under federal and state healthcare laws and other laws.

Providers are increasingly being challenged to establish that relationships are at fair market value. The failure to establish fair market value can have the following implications:

- Loss of federal income tax exception: Payment in excess of fair market value can result in inurement/private benefit, resulting in:

  Loss of exemption, potential spillover to tax-exempt affiliates

  Payment of taxes

  Loss of tax-exempt status of bonds

- Intermediate sanctions. Payment of consideration in excess of fair market value in a transaction to a disqualified person is an excess benefit transaction resulting in excise taxes on the disqualified person and the organization managers.

- Violation of the antikickback statute: Payment in excess of fair market value generally means that no safe harbor exists and that there is a presumption that the excess payment is in consideration of referrals. This can violate Medicare/Medicaid antireferral provisions resulting in:

Five years' imprisonment, $25,000 fine

Exclusion from Medicare/Medicaid

Civil monetary penalties of up to $50,000 plus three times the amount of damages (added by Health Insurance Portability & Accountability Act of 1996)

- Violation of Stark laws: Payment in excess of fair market value can result in a structure where a physician cannot refer to a hospital or its affiliate for designated health services, and the hospital or other entity cannot bill or collect for such services.
- Contract issues: Payment in excess of fair market value that violates the Stark or antikickback statute can void a contract based on illegality.
- Beyond the scope of the public body (in the case of a transaction by a public hospital or other public entity): Payment in excess of fair market value exceeds the scope of the public, resulting in the potential for:

Personal liability of trustees

Taxpayer suit

Injunction

Acceptable compensation is established by the existence of the following:

- The total compensation package is reasonable.
- It is the result of arm's-length bargaining.
- It is not a disguised dividend or other device to distribute profits and does not convert the essential nature of an organization into a joint venture.
- It is properly reported by the exempt organization for tax purposes.
- It does not violate other laws such that the violation results in the exempt organization engaging in a substantial nonexempt activity.

Obviously, opportunities exist in physician-hospital integration models to consolidate and control costs. Laboratory and radiology services are just two examples that may provide economies of scale for the practice and the hospital. However, extreme care should be taken to ensure that patients are billed appropriately.

For example, assume that the hospital and medical office decide to consolidate laboratory services. The medical office closes its in-office laboratory facilities, and all testing is performed at the hospital. If the laboratory tests are billed from the medical office, the government may be able to demonstrate that the medical group has violated the federal False Claims Act (FCA), since claims were submitted to the government for services performed by another provider in violation of federal law. Additionally, the medical group could be in violation of the state antimarkup laws, which typically contain disclosure requirements if laboratory work is not performed by the billing entity.

The challenge of this type of model is to operate the medical practice office as an ambulatory practice. Hospital administration skills are not transferable to medical practices. In order to be successful, the hospital owner must develop the processes and policies necessary to manage a medical practice successfully. The hospital must be able to bill and collect efficiently and provide for knowledgeable on-site management. Inefficient management can quickly unravel the hospital-owned physician practice model.

The most difficult issue in the hospital-physician integration process is that of physician compensation. More than likely, physicians of the acquired group will experience a change in the way they are compensated. It is possible that the affiliation will cause long-standing disputes regarding group compensation to surface.

The group must understand and accept that any change in the compensation system is likely to create winners and losers. It is imperative to the success of the integrated entity that financial models be constructed that will forecast physician compensation in the new arrangement. Identifying the winners and losers in advance and making the appropriate modifications prior to implementation of the model is critical. The models created should accurately reflect various scenarios for discussion prior to affiliation.

CHAPTER EIGHTEEN

Compensating the Physician CEO

Leading physicians is like herding cats!
—Unknown

Every physician reveres the tradition of the physician leader. The physician leader was typically a physician who excelled at patient care, teaching, research, and administration and served as mentor to others. The concept of CEO or medical director, which is less than twenty years old, was founded in this tradition of leadership.

With the rapid change in the healthcare field, effective leadership is becoming increasingly important for practice organizations and the people they serve. When physicians accept leadership responsibilities, they become responsible for molding the practice team, setting direction, and teaching others.

Leadership is focused on producing needed change. Leaders define what the future should look like, align people with that vision, and inspire them to make it happen regardless of obstacles and setbacks. Physician leaders must be willing to trade some portion of medicine for administration. They must be concerned, visionary, communicative, focused, patient, credible, and compassionate.

Effective leaders should have the ability to:

- Initiate change. Leaders examine the current situation and look ahead to future possibilities. Effective leaders are able to recognize the need for change and have the ability to direct change.

- Define reality. Effective leaders define reality through their ability to collect and analyze data. They are able to discern facts clearly and communicate accordingly.
- Maintain courage. Leaders are able to take the risk of failure associated with proposing change.
- Communicate well. The ability to communicate well may be the single most important trait of a physician leader. An effective leader must develop the ability to deliver bad news (i.e., explaining to a physician member that his or her performance is below standard).
- Persuade. An effective leader is able to maintain credibility and is persistent in describing the benefits of moving from the status quo to a desired future state.
- Handle criticism. One dissenter can derail a worthwhile project. Leaders listen to all voices and then must bring the group to action despite heavy criticism from within the group itself.
- Maintain respect. Physician leaders receive a mantle of leadership from their colleagues on the basis of the belief that they are excellent physicians and are trustworthy, confident, articulate, and willing to admit mistakes.
- Take action. Leadership is a process, and an effective leader must be able to initiate change.

Leaders exist only in relation to the people they lead. If there are leaders, there must be followers. Following is not a natural act for physicians, who are trained to be independent thinkers. Leading physicians has been compared to herding cats. In order for the physician leader to be effective, the physicians he or she leads must be willing to follow.

As followers, physicians in a group practice must be willing to:

- Participate. Leaders want and need ideas, criticism, and opinions. Organizations are directed by those who show up and stay until the vote is taken.
- Maintain a positive attitude. The best team members can analyze problems, contribute to solutions, and participate in the change process while maintaining a positive attitude. Some degree of skepticism is healthy; however, a constant pessimist can be a destructive force in an organization.

- Be honest. Team members must be able to state their views and opinions honestly. Although this is not usually a problem for physicians, they may choose to state their views in the doctor's lounge, not at group board meetings.
- Be respectful. Members of the group must be able to state their opinion without attacking the individual.
- Be responsible. Practice members cannot expect the leader to solve all group problems alone. Leaders do not have all the answers. Members of the group must be willing to contribute to the solution.
- Be a team player. Unfortunately, group medical practices often are paralyzed by the fear of offending one loud negative member. The fear may result in a lack of action being taken on an important issue. Members of the group must agree to operate in a democracy. They must be willing to state their views and then accept and support the decision of the group.

Physician leaders are faced with challenges unique to the practice of medicine. They must be able to lead individuals who are taught to be independent critical thinkers. As such, physicians may tend to overanalyze a situation to the point that action is stifled.

Additionally, physicians are skilled craftsmen who are proud of their ability to treat each patient in a customized way. Their craftsman role may make them resistant to any change that is perceived to affect their skill and judgement.

Occasionally, tension may exist between the practice administrator and the physician CEO or medical director. The administrator may see the medical director as an "amateur" in the field of practice business and may resent the input of the physician leader. Similarly, the physician leader may view the administrator as an obstacle to be overcome. This tension can sabotage real improvement because almost all improvements require cooperation between the two. Physicians and administrators must respect each other's role and trust each other's ability to do their job effectively.

The division of labor between the physician leader and the practice administrator will vary from practice to practice. In some cases, the administrator will handle virtually everything, only communicating the overall plan and any related problems with the physician leader. In still other situations, the administrator and physician leader may share common duties.

In order for a sharing of duties to work, there must be a clear division of responsibilities between the physician leader and the administrator. In some cases, it may be wise for the practice to bring in an independent consultant to assist in establishing specific roles. In most small to medium-size practices, the physician leader will still have to practice medicine, most possibly with a reduced schedule. The amount of time devoted to practicing medicine will depend on the specific duties assigned along with the size of the practice.

Likewise, physician leaders must be able to accept that they are not members of the group anymore. They may be practicing medicine, but they are also managers, and that may create some dissent with and distance from other physicians in the group. Physician leaders must accept this reality while not forgetting what it was like to be a member of the group in the trenches.

Physician leaders may be reluctant to exercise the necessary power required to lead in certain situations. As a rule, physicians are reluctant to go against the professional autonomy of their colleagues. In such situations, it is important for the physician leader to remember that nothing destroys a medical organization faster than persistent tolerance of incompetence or indifference in the face of controversy. As painful as it may be, a physician leader must be able to use his or her power of leadership in appropriate situations. Otherwise, morale and quality will suffer.

Many physicians continue to visualize themselves as scientists. As such, the concept of business entrepreneur is still foreign and perhaps distasteful to them. Physician leaders must be able to face new opportunities and reinvent themselves as physician executives and entrepreneurs.

Although there is a need and demand for physician leadership, many people are thrust into the leadership role without any formal training in medical management. These individuals are trying to create a bridge between two professions. Physicians already have an understanding of the clinical side of the practice, but to be a leader it is necessary to develop the knowledge and skills of management.

Physician leaders should pursue education through self-study and/or leadership classes in the following areas:

- Finance: Physician leaders should have a basic understanding of financial reporting. They should be able to read and understand a balance sheet and income statement.

- General business: Training in the areas of marketing, market research, strategic planning, and contract negotiation is important for the physician leader.

- Managed care: Physician leaders must understand the basics of managed care and how it affects practice operations.

- Team building and communication: Physician leaders should self-assess their communications skill set. Communicating, interacting, and team building are important leadership skills.

- Clinical improvement: An effective physician leader must be able to direct the group in quality and utilization issues through the effective use of data and research.

Formal training in business ensures that physician leaders play on a level field with business administrators. Increasing numbers of physicians are opting for training in business school. Some medical schools now offer combined MD/MBA degrees. Physicians dedicated to a career in management are the ones most likely to benefit from an MBA.

The emergence of the CEO is symbolic of the change in the physician's role. Physicians are taking leadership roles in group practices with a variety of assigned duties. Physician leaders may continue to provide healthcare services on a reduced schedule.

The physician CEO is responsible for the overall operation of the organization, including patient care and contract negotiations. This individual develops and monitors organizational policy in conjunction with other management personnel and the organization's board of directors. The physician CEO oversees activities that relate to the future growth of the organization (strategic planning and marketing) and generally serves as a liaison between the organization and constituents, such as staff members, businesses, and individuals in the community.

The medical director must be a licensed physician. The position typically includes both clinical and administrative duties. The medical director is responsible for all activities related to the delivery of medical care and clinical services (i.e., cost management, utilization review, quality assurance, and medical protocol development). Likewise, the medical director typically oversees the activities of group physicians, including recruiting and credentialing. The medical director usually reports to the physician CEO or the governing board of the practice.

Duties of the medical director may include medical administration, evaluation and management of physicians, committee responsibilities, quality management, and miscellaneous.

MEDICAL ADMINISTRATION

- Analyze and evaluate the functioning of medical staff. Report regularly to the board of directors on the activities of the medical staff and the performance of its various components, including making recommendations for appropriate actions to help see that the activities of the medical staff are in conformance with the objectives established by the board of directors.
- Attend all meetings of the board of directors in an ex officio capacity.
- Perform other duties as requested by the board of directors, including ad hoc handling of problems relating to the practice of medicine and patient care.
- Develop and implement a physician scheduling system. Monitor physician schedules, vacations, and continuing medical education (CME) time.

EVALUATION AND MANAGEMENT OF PHYSICIANS

- Establish and maintain an ongoing program to orient and evaluate new physicians. Meet at least quarterly with all first-year physicians. Maintain appropriate records and report to the board of directors on any major problems.
- Establish and maintain performance evaluation program for all physicians. Maintain appropriate records and report to the board of directors on any major problems.
- Evaluate physician compliance with practice standards, protocols, pathways, and the like. Take corrective action as necessary.
- See that prompt action is taken when evidence of incompetence or negligence is presented regarding a provider.
- Intervene and mediate all major physician-physician, physician-patient, and, in conjunction with the administrator, physician-staff concerns as needed. Work with administrative staff to promote cordial relationships among physicians, patients, and staff. Act on patients' complaints regarding dissatisfaction with physicians. De-

termine if the complaint is founded or unfounded. Maintain appropriate records, and document the issues dealt with and their resolutions.

- Carry out disciplinary actions upon medical staff members as determined by the board of directors or within the independent latitudes and discretion afforded by the board.

COMMITTEE RESPONSIBILITIES

- Work as needed with standing medical staff committees and serve as ex officio member of all medical staff committees.
- Participate in physician recruiting activities, including interviewing candidates.
- Regularly attend departmental meetings. Provide input, direction, and guidance as needed.

QUALITY MANAGEMENT

- Oversee, through the department chairman and committee structure, the development and implementation of practice standards, protocols, pathways, and outcomes management.
- Develop and implement patient management and utilization review activties.

MISCELLANEOUS DUTIES

- Serve as physician liaison in dealing with the board of directors and the administrative staff.
- Represent the practice in its relationships with outside organizations in matters relating to the practice of medicine and patient care.
- Attain and maintain familiarity with medical-moral and medical-legal issues relating to the practice of medicine. Serve as a resource for the medical staff in related matters.
- Assist administrative staff in risk control programs. Review all potential liability claims against the practice.
- Review the minutes of all applicable committee meetings.

According to the Medical Group Management Association 1999 Report, physician CEOs have experienced a 20.41 percent increase in compensation from 1994 to 1998 ($215,286 to $259,231). Conversely, medical directors have experienced a 0.07 percent drop in compensation ($160,116 to $160,000). Compensation for medical directors peaked in 1997 with a high compensation for the period 1994 to 1998 of $186,720.

According to the MGMA survey, physician CEOs commanded a higher salary in a group practice ($295,774) than in a hospital/health system ($252,137). The opposite is true for medical directors. In the hospital setting, the median compensation for a medical director is $165,000 while in group practice the median compensation is $160,000.

Median compensation for physician CEOs in single-specialty practices exceeds their multispecialty counterparts ($318,098 versus $249,897). Compensation likewise declines as the percent of capitated revenue increases. Practices with no capitation reflected median compensation of $285,369 while practices with 51 percent or more capitation reflected median compensation of $252,137. Interestingly, practices with less than $20,000,000 in revenue reflected a higher median than practices with revenue in excess of $20,000,000 ($278,928 versus 254,274).

In contrast to the physician CEO compensation, medical director respondents to the MGMA survey faired better in multispecialty than in single specialty practices. The median compensation for medical directors in multispecialty practices was $169,798 as compared with $137,674 for single-specialty practices. Unlike their physician CEO counterparts compensation for medical directors increased with the amount of practice revenue. Practices with revenues under $20,000,000 reflected median medical director compensation of $139,403 while practices with revenues in excess of $20,000,000 reported median compensation of $172,302. Additionally, medical director compensation increases proportionately with the increase in managed care revenues. Practices with no capitation reflected median compensation of $138,066 while practices with 11 to 50 percent capitation indicated a median of $165,100.

The medical director's role may be full time or part time depending on the size of the practice and the duties assigned. According to the MGMA study, income increased proportionately with the percentage of time spent on administrative duties. For example, medical directors who spent 50 to 70 percent of their time on administrative duties received a median salary of $139,403 while medical directors who spent 91 percent or more of their time on administrative duties received a median compensation of $170,003.

If the physician participates as a medical director on a part-time basis, the practice can apportion a reasonable salary for the duties and time commitment as medical director and adjust the base salary accordingly.

For example, assume that a multispecialty group assigns the duties of the medical director to one of its family practice members and that the duties of medical director will constitute one-half of the office day. In other words, the physician will be allocated four hours of the workday for medical director duties, and patient scheduling will be adjusted accordingly for the remaining half of the day. The practice sets a base salary for family practice physicians at $140,000. Assume that the amount established as compensation for the medical director's position is set at $85,000. The base salary for the medical director would be computed as follows:

Medical directorship	$85,000
Base salary ($140,000 × 50%)	70,000
Total base compensation	$155,000

CHAPTER NINETEEN

Physician
Compensation Case Studies

Designing or redesigning physician compensation plans can produce tension and resistance in the group practice. With any compensation plan, there are winners and losers. The self-perception of fair typically results in the winners believing in the equity of the formula while those who lose ground in the new computation have the inherent fear that the plan is somehow unfair.

The goal of plan design is to appeal to the overall equity of the system. Base compensation should be defined based on the competitive market while requiring the achievement of certain minimum standards. Expenses should be analyzed carefully, independent of the formula, to define those expenses that vary with volume and those that remain fixed. The incentive calculation should be designed to promote behaviors that support the group's mission and goals. By addressing and gaining consensus on these broad concepts prior to performing the what's-in-it-for-me calculation, the group may be guided to a group concept of equity and fairness.

In a perfect world, equal compensation would be the preferred design—one for all and all for one. Equal compensation certainly would promote the "team" concept and reduce any negative competitiveness. And, in fact, equal compensation works well for hospital-based physicians who basically work on a schedule (i.e., radiology, pathology, anesthesiology).

With the exception of hospital-based practices, however, equal compensation can be a disincentive to excellence. Each physician brings to the practice a certain skill set that benefits the overall group. Equal compensation assumes that each physician has a similar skill set and similar work ethic. In reality, this does not exist. A compensation model based on equal compensation provides a negative environment for both the underachiever, who must constantly defend his or her work product, and the overachiever, who is constantly feeling cheated.

Designing or redesigning a compensation model can promote tension in the practice as all physicians seek to protect their self-interest. Establishing the basic principles of plan design (base salary, overhead allocation, incentive pool) will negate some of the anxiety but will not eliminate the defensiveness created when a physician realizes that his or her compensation may be reduced under the new formula.

Defensiveness can result in hostile behavior. Lines can be drawn between offices in multisite practices and between specialties in multispecialty practices. In one case, a multispecialty internal medicine practice became so deadlocked over the redesign of their compensation formula that the administrator recommended that the physicians cash a check for the available funds at the end of the month, stack the cash in the parking lot, and fight over it. The analogy pointed out the pettiness of the group and refocused the physicians on designing a plan that would promote the group's mission and establish overall equity.

Physicians must be included in the design process and must be guided to consensus based on the achievement of group goals. If the group goals are met, income should increase accordingly. As the size of the pie increases, each piece of the pie increases proportionately, no matter how it is cut. The plan should focus the activities of the group's individual physicians on those actions that will increase the revenue pool for everyone.

The following case studies provide sample situations that may be encountered in plan design. In each case, the respective group strives to achieve equity and regulatory compliance while maintaining the incentives to encourage individual productivity.

CASE 1: ABC INTERNAL MEDICINE PRACTICE

Facts: ABC Internal Medicine Practice is a group practice comprised of three physicians. The physicians merged their solo practices five years ago in order to obtain economies of scale and to be able to negotiate effectively with managed care payors. Dr. A is a pulmonary subspecialist, Dr. B is an endocrinologist, and Dr. C practices general internal medicine.

The practice provides radiology and laboratory services (both designated health services under Stark II). The existing compensation formula is based on an eat-what-you-kill mentality. In the past, each physician has been credited with his respective collections from all patient services, including radiology and laboratory. Dr. A and Dr. B are the highest users of radiology and laboratory services based on their subspecialties.

The physicians have been pleased with their current system of compensation. They have analyzed overhead and feel they have appropriately allocated expenses between fixed and variable designations. Due to their subspecialty designations, a direct allocation of income is deemed to be a fair basis of compensation.

Objective: The physicians and their advisors were unaware of the Stark regulations as they relate to physician compensation formulas. Since the designated health services were provided in the group practice, the physicians incorrectly assumed that they were in total compliance with Stark.

The group wants to revise its compensation plan for the upcoming fiscal year to be in compliance with Stark regulations. The physicians understand that, in order to be in compliance, the revised plan will not directly allocate designated health service revenues (radiology and laboratory) to the physicians who ordered the services. Their goal is to develop a plan that will comply with Stark while maintaining, to some degree, their existing compensation levels.

Existing Plan: The existing compensation plan provides for a direct allocation of physician collections (including radiology and laboratory collections). Expenses are divided as follows:

1. $25,000 in expenses are allocated equally to each physician (fixed expenses).
2. The balance of expenses is allocated based on the percentage of individual collections by physician to total group collections.

The formula produced the following results for the current year:

	Evaluation & Management Collections	Ancillary Collections	Total	Fixed Overhead	Variable Overhead	Net
Dr. A	$400,000	$50,000	$450,000	$25,000	$222,000	$203,000
Dr. B	375,000	85,000	460,000	25,000	228,000	207,000
Dr. C	375,000	30,000	405,000	25,000	200,000	180,000
Total	$1,150,000	$165,000	$1,315,000	$75,000	$650,000	$590,000

Alternative I: Equal Sharing of Designated Health Services Revenues

In the first alternative, all collections from designated health services (radiology and laboratory) were pooled and were allocated equally to each physician. Expenses were allocated in accordance with the existing formula

($25,000 equally, the balance based on a percentage of individual collections to total collections). Variable expenses are allocated based on the revised total collections (with designated health services allocated equally).

Applying the assumptions in the first alternative compensation plan to the current year's numbers resulted in the following:

	Evaluation & Management Collections	Ancillary Collections	Total	Fixed Overhead	Variable Overhead	Net
Dr. A	$400,000	$55,000	$455,000	$25,000	$224,000	$206,000
Dr. B	375,000	55,000	430,000	25,000	213,000	192,000
Dr. C	375,000	55,000	430,000	25,000	213,000	192,000
Total	$1,150,000	$165,000	$1,315,000	$75,000	$650,000	$590,000

Dividing designated health services revenues equally results in a shift in compensation from Dr. B (previously the highest-compensated physician) to Dr. C (previously the lowest-compensated physician.

Compensation shifts due to an equal sharing of the designated health service revenue are as follows:

	Existing Formula	Alternative I	Increase (Decrease)
Dr. A	$203,000	$206,000	$3,000
Dr. B	207,000	192,000	(15,000)
Dr. C	180,000	192,000	12,000

The group's reaction to Alternative I is not favorable. Although the group goal is to develop a compensation model that will be in compliance with the Stark regulations, the dramatic shift in income from Dr. B to Dr. C is not acceptable. The group has even discussed splitting up if another alternative cannot be developed.

Alternative II: Allocation of Designated Health Services Based on Evaluation and Management Revenue

The Stark regulations provide that revenues from designated health services cannot be allocated, for compensation purposes, directly to the physician who ordered the services. The revenues may be pooled and allocated equally (as in Alternative I) or by some other method as long as they are not allocated directly to the ordering physician.

A reasonable alternative may be to allocate the designated health services based on the respective evaluation and management service revenues of the individual physicians. For simplicity in this example we have used collections. However, a more exact allocation would result from evaluation and management charges. In the case of multispecialty practices (i.e., surgical and primary care combinations), an allocation of designated health service revenue based on evaluation and management charges may provide for a reasonable allocation of income.

Reallocating radiology and laboratory revenues based on evaluation and management revenue in Alternative II results in the following distribution based on current year numbers:

	Evaluation & Management Collections	Ancillary Collections	Total	Fixed Overhead	Variable Overhead	Net
Dr. A	$400,000	$57,000	$457,000	$25,000	$226,000	$206,000
Dr. B	375,000	54,000	429,000	25,000	212,000	192,000
Dr. C	375,000	54,000	429,000	25,000	212,000	192,000
Total	$1,150,000	$165,000	$1,315,000	$75,000	$650,000	$590,000

The results of Alternative II are identical to Alternative I. Dr. B's ordering of ancillaries is much greater than Dr. C's ordering based on his subspecialty of endocrinology. An allocation of designated health services based on evaluation and management revenues may produce no effect in situations where the designated health service revenue is disproportionate to evaluation and management revenue based on differences in the combined specialties. The same situation might occur if the practice included an oncologist with significant in-office chemotherapy revenues.

Alternative III: Establishing a Base Salary

The first two alternatives have not resulted in a viable formula for the group. Although the group has traditionally maintained an eat-what-you-kill mentality, the establishment of a base salary may be necessary to achieve compliance and maintain the integrity of the group.

The Stark regulations allow the establishment of a base amount as long as the amount is determined in advance. Alternative III provides for the establishment of a base salary equal to 80 percent of the total current year compensation determined as follows:

	Current Year Compensation	Base at 80%
Dr. A	$203,000	$163,000
Dr. B	207,000	167,000
Dr. C	180,000	145,000
Total	$590,000	$475,000

The incentive pool available for allocation (based on current year's numbers) is computed as follows:

Total collections	$1,315,000
Less: total overhead	(725,000)
Less: total physician base salaries	(475,000)
Incentive pool	$115,000

The incentive pool then is allocated based on each physician's respective share of evaluation and management revenue to the total as follows:

	Evaluation & Management Revenue %	Share of Incentive Pool
Dr. A	34%	$40,000
Dr. B	33%	38,000
Dr. C	33%	38,000
Total		$115,000

Combining the incentive pool with the established base salaries results in the following total compensation per physician (based on current year numbers):

	Base Salary	Incentive	Total
Dr. A	$163,000	$39,000	$202,000
Dr. B	167,000	38,000	205,000
Dr. C	145,000	38,000	183,000
Total	$475,000	$115,000	$590,000

Alternative III compares to the existing formula as follows:

	Existing Formula	Alternative III
Dr. A	$203,000	$202,000
Dr. B	207,000	205,000
Dr. C	180,000	183,000

Although Alternative III requires a shift in group mentality from the eat-what-you-kill methodology, the physicians are willing to make that shift to maintain the integrity of their income. Alternative III provides a way to establish a Stark-compliant compensation formula while achieving the group distribution goals.

The following items must be considered in establishing a base compensation plan:

- The base salary should not exceed 80 percent of total expected compensation.
- The base salary should be comparative with the market based on the physician's specialty, tenure, and qualifications.
- The base salary is set in advance and should not be modified during the computation year simply to accommodate the formula. If factors change (i.e., a physician reduces hours to a part-time status), then the base can be revised. The formula should incorporate standard objectives that should be achieved in order to "earn" the established base. If these objectives are not being met, the base can be revised. Otherwise, it should remain in effect until the next computation period.

Case 1 illustrates the fact that the practice must consider several alternatives to ensure that its goals are achieved and that appropriate incentives are in place. Unfortunately, no existing formula will work in all practices. Designing an effective compensation plan requires a thorough knowledge of the practice goals and objectives as well as the applicable regulations that impact the formula.

CASE 2: XYZ SURGICAL GROUP

Facts: XYZ Surgical group consists of three general surgeons. The physicians operate as a professional corporation and are located in a single medical office. The practice was established by Physician X in 1972. Physician Y joined in 1980, and Physician Z joined the practice in 1990.

When Dr. Y joined the practice in 1980, the compensation plan was established. The practice provides for a monthly draw that is applied against an annual computation. The computation takes the net income from the practice and divides 50 percent of the net income equally among the physicians. The remaining 50 percent is divided based on each physician's collections as a percentage of total collections. Obviously, over the years the cost of operating the practice has increased and reimbursement from third-party payors has declined.

Because of his reputation and tenure, Dr. X generated the largest volume of cases for many years. When Dr. Z joined the practice in 1990, Dr. X began to reduce his caseload. Over the past 10 years, Dr. Z's caseload and revenues have increased, those of Dr. Y have remained approximately the same, and those of Dr. X have declined.

Recently Dr. X announced that, as a move toward retirement, he would like to drop out of the call rotation. Dr. X would like his compensation reduced to compensate for his reduction in schedule.

Objective: The current formula has been under scrutiny for a couple of years by Dr. Z, who has seen his income increase while his compensation has not increased proportionately.

The group wants to revise its current compensation formula to provide for:

- Dr. X's reduction in schedule
- Continued equal sharing of some portion of revenue based on being a participant in the group
- Commensurate rewards for revenue generated

Existing Plan

The existing plan provides for an equal sharing of 50 percent of the net income of the practice with the remaining 50 percent shared based on a percentage of the individual physician's collections to total collections.

Practice income for the prior year was as follows:

	Charges	%	RVUs	%	Collections	%
Dr. X	$850,000	20%	6,300	21%	$350,000	20%
Dr. Y	1,200,000	28%	8,200	28%	570,000	32%
Dr. Z	2,150,000	52%	15,000	51%	850,000	48%
	$4,200,000		29,500		$1,770,000	

Net income for the prior year was as follows:

Collections	$1,770,000	
Overhead	530,000	(30%)
Net income before MD compensation	$1,240,000	

Compensation based on the existing formula was computed as follows:

	50% equal share	50% based on collections	Total
Dr. X	$206,000	$124,000	$330,000
Dr Y.	206,000	199,000	405,000
Dr. Z	206,000	299,000	505,000
Total	$618,000	$622,000	$1,240,000

A review of the existing formula based on the prior year's financial results revealed several inconsistencies. First, the percentage of individual compensation using the existing formula was markedly different from the individual percentage of individual physician revenue, especially between Dr. X and Dr. Y. (The practice has no designated health services revenue.)

	% Charges	% RVUs	% Collections	% Compensation
Dr. X	20%	21%	20%	27%
Dr. Y	28%	28%	32%	33%
Dr. Z	52%	51%	48%	40%

The current formula likewise resulted in a skewing of the allocation of practice overhead. Although the overhead percentage for the practice was approximately 30 percent, the formula resulted in the following allocation of overhead:

	Collections	Compensation	Overhead	%
Dr. X	$350,000	$330,000	$20,000	6%
Dr. Y	570,000	405,000	165,000	29%
Dr. Z	850,000	505,000	345,000	41%
Total	$1,770,000	$1,240,000	$530,000	

After reviewing the inconsistencies of the existing formula, regardless of Dr. X's decision not to take calls, the physicians agreed that a total overhaul was in order.

Step One: Establish Base Compensation

The physicians agreed that a portion of their compensation should be guaranteed based on their participation in and employment by the practice. In anticipation of recruiting additional surgeons in the future, they wanted the base to be competitive. The physicians agreed to use the median compensation for a general surgeon as reflected in the Medical Group Management Association's 1999 Report in the base salary calculation. The total median compensation amount reflected in the survey was $225,653. The base for a full-time surgeon with call coverage duties was set at 80 percent of the median total compensation for a general surgeon, $180,000. Drs. Y and Z's base compensation was set at $180,000.

Much discussion ensued regarding the calculation for a base compensation amount for Dr. X. A review of Dr. X's current productivity indicated that he was below the median RVUs for a general surgeon as reflected in the MGMA's 1999 Report (6,300 RVUs versus the median of 7,375). Additionally, Drs. Y and Z considered Dr. X's withdrawal from the call coverage rotation to be a substantial reduction in his group contribution. The physicians ultimately agreed that a 75 percent reduction from the full-time base was reasonable for Dr. X based on the circumstances. Dr. X's base salary was set at $135,000.

Step Two: Allocate Overhead

The review of the existing formula pointed out the great disparity in overhead allocation. The practice overhead was approximately 30 percent overall, the amount allocated to Dr. X based on the formula was 6 percent whereas the amount allocated to Dr. Z was 41 percent.

The physicians agreed to designate expenses as fixed (allocated equally among the physicians regardless of productivity) and variable (allocated to the physicians based on their individual productivity). A review of expenses for the prior year indicated that approximately 40 percent of the expenses were fixed and 60 percent were variable.

The practice fee schedule was not based on RVUs, although, charge volume was commensurate to the RVUs by physician. In order to convert productivity to RVUs, the practice used schedules produced by the billing system. The schedules provided the frequency of charges by physician by CPT code for the prior year. The practice then applied the physician work RVUs as reported in the *Federal Register* (Appendix C) to the frequency of the CPT codes performed by physician to compute total work RVUs. The physicians agreed to use RVUs to allocate variable expenses.

Using the agreed fixed and variable ratios with the prior year's overhead resulted in the following allocation:

	Fixed	Variable (based on RVUs)	Total
Dr. X	$71,000	$68,000	$139,000
Dr. Y	71,000	88,000	159,000
Dr. Z	71,000	161,000	232,000
Total	$213,000	$317,000	$530,000

Step Three: Establish Basis for Incentive Revenue

The physicians agreed that practice success was dependent on physician productivity and as such agreed to use RVUs as the basis to assign incentive revenues. The incentive revenue pool was determined as follows:

Total practice collections	$1,770,000
Physician base compensation	495,000
Incentive revenue pool	$1,275,000

Based on individual physician RVUs, the incentive revenue pool was assigned as follows:

	RVUs	Share of Incentive Pool
Dr. X	6,300	$268,000
Dr. Y	8,200	357,000
Dr. Z	15,000	650,000
Total	29,500	$1,275,000

Step Four: Compute the Incentive Bonus

The incentive bonus is computed based on incentive revenue allocated by RVUs less expenses allocated as agreed (fixed and variable).

	Incentive Revenue	Less: Allocated Expenses	Net
Dr. X	$268,000	$139,000	$129,000
Dr. Y	357,000	159,000	198,000
Dr. Z	650,000	232,000	418,000
Total	$1,275,000	$530,000	$745,000

Total compensation for the physicians for the prior year based on the proposed formula would be as follows:

	Base Salary	Incentive Bonus	Total	%
Dr. X	$135,000	$129,000	$264,000	21%
Dr. Y	180,000	198,000	378,000	30%
Dr. Z	180,000	418,000	598,000	49%
Total	$495,000	$745,000	$1,240,000	

The proposed formula compares with the existing formula as follows:

	% of Existing Formula	% of Proposed Formula	% of RVUs
Dr. X	27%	21%	21%
Dr. Y	33%	30%	28%
Dr. Z	40%	49%	51%

The proposed formula (applied to the prior year's financial results) provided the practice with the following:

- A base salary computation based on market values for general surgery
- A method to reduce compensation for physicians, such as Dr. X, who desire to reduce their work schedule
- An allocation of expenses based on fixed and variable amounts
- Incentive allocation by RVUs
- Total compensation that aligns the physician's compensation with his or her contribution to the group

CHAPTER TWENTY

Common Pitfalls

A journey of 1000 miles must begin with a single step.
—Chinese proverb

Pitfalls are inherent in the establishment of a group compensation model for a medical practice. Whether the group has an existing plan it wishes to revise or a new group is forming and needs to develop a plan, change creates insecurity. There will be winners and losers in the development of any compensation model. The financial changes in the healthcare industry combined with the current regulatory requirements can make plan design tricky. If not properly planned and communicated, the compensation model itself can be the death knell for a group practice.

A well-designed compensation model should:

- Promote group goals
- Provide appropriate incentives
- Promote group financial stability
- Be competitive in the market

Unfortunately, while attempting to meet these objectives, certain pitfalls can result. The first occurs when the group establishes a plan that provides for bonuses in excess of profits. In an attempt to pacify group members and minimize the compensation "losers," the plan can provide for compensation levels in excess of net income. When a compensation model allows physicians to overdraw their amount due, the tendency may be to finance the shortfall in hopes that the situation will be self-correcting.

The following example is a simple illustration:

	Compensation Due Based on Group Formula	Base Salary	Net Due
Dr. A	$150,000	$160,000	($10,000)
Dr. B	170,000	160,000	10,000
Total	$320,000	$320,000	

In this scenario, the practice has paid Dr. B's $10,000 bonus to Dr. A. The administrator is faced with a real dilemma. On one hand, she can ask Dr. A to pay back the $10,000 he has been overpaid so that the practice will have the funds to pay Dr. B's bonus (not a particularly attractive alternative). Or she can recommend that the practice borrow the funds to pay Dr. B's bonus and hope that next year will work out better.

This example may seem far-fetched; however, it happens all too often. The moral of the story is that base salaries always should be set well below (at least 20 percent below) anticipated compensation. Doing so provides an adequate cushion for incentive calculations. Additionally, physician performance should be monitored during the computation period. If a physician is not achieving the standard required for the level of base salary received, adjustments should be considered before the incentive is calculated.

Another common pitfall occurs when the compensation plan incorporates incentives that do not support group incentives. Good incentive plans can enable the practice to improve performance and achieve overall financial success. If the individual incentives are not aligned properly with group incentives, the practice may suffer.

For instance, if the compensation formula is tied totally to individual physician productivity, physicians may be discouraged from sharing patient volume within the group. This situation can be disastrous for practices that are attempting to grow by adding new physicians. The new physicians may have empty schedules while established physicians have long wait times for appointments.

Common pitfalls in incentive plan design may include the following:

- A plan that encourages the physicians to believe they are entitled to bonuses in spite of their performance or the financial situation of the group
- An incentive plan that provides for insignificant rewards (i.e., base salaries set too high)
- Incentives that are not clearly linked to the achievement
- Incentive formulas that are overly complicated and not understood

An incentive plan must include the necessary benchmarks that will allow the medical group practice to reach its stated goals. Remember, what is measured usually is what gets done.

An inappropriate allocation of expenses can result in the establishment of disincentives to productivity. If practice overhead is allocated totally based on physician revenue, then all risk is removed. If physicians have no revenue, then they likewise have no expense. Overhead should be allocated between those expenses that are fixed (do not vary with patient volume) and those that are variable (vary with patient volume). The establishment of a certain portion of equal share expenses (fixed overhead) will encourage productivity.

Last, an inappropriate allocation of designated health service income in a group practice can result in serious financial consequences. The practice must be aware of all regulatory requirements regarding physician compensation plans. A disregard for established government regulations, such as the Stark regulations, can result in serious financial penalties. Noncompliance with Stark can result in a $100,000 penalty per noncompliant agreement. Additionally, the practice can be excluded from the Medicare and Medicaid program.

When there is plenty of money, almost any plan will work; when there is not enough money, almost no plan will work. Too often groups wait too late to analyze the effects of their income distribution plan. If income is dropping for everyone, the financial analysis involved with developing a new system usually identifies financial issues that the group either has not been informed of or chose to ignore. Obviously, financial crisis complicates the issue.

Sample Physician Encounter Budget and Comparison

Ambulatory Encounters Budgeted/Month	MGMA Median	MGMA 75th	MTD Actual	YTD Actual	YTD Variance
500	389	485	318	2,253	(747)
500	389	485	314	2,311	(689)
375	389	485	498	1,503	(747)
375	389	485	163	920	(1,350)
500	389	485	621	3,018	18
415	389	485	291	2,203	(287)
500	389	485	380	2,704	(296)
500	389	485	379	2,669	(331)
	389	485	348	599	599
320	281	353	166	1,095	(825)
320	281	353	302	1,683	(237)
224	199	251	215	1,293	(51)
128	81	102	96	821	53
320	281	353	221	1,403	(517)
320	281	353	317	1,881	(39)
320	281	353	228	1,379	(541)
480	410	507	468	3,038	158
	410	507	277	933	933
				715	715
480	410	507	260	2,417	(463)
480	410	507	401	2,526	(354)
480	410	507	225	2,253	(627)
480	410	507	295	2,705	(175)
480	410	507	260	2,396	(484)
528	410	507	464	3,323	155
480	410	507	324	2,939	59

Sample Practice Budget

	Jan	Feb	Mar	Apr	May	June	July	Aug
Gross Charges	80,652	88,727	89,404	75,696	80,576	88,546	66,904	70,704
Collection %	82.00%	82.00%	82.00%	82.00%	82.00%	82.00%	82.00%	82.00%
Collections	66,135	72,756	73,311	62,070	66,072	72,607	54,861	57,977
Less: Refunds	(661)	(728)	(733)	(621)	(661)	(726)	(549)	(580)
Net Revenues	65,474	72,028	72,578	61,450	65,411	71,881	54,312	57,398
Site Operating Expenses:								
Personnel								
Expenses	13,400	13,400	13,400	13,400	20,101	13,400	12,321	12,321
Occupancy								
Costs	5,382	5,382	5,382	5,382	4,734	4,734	4,734	4,734
Medical Expenses	4,341	4,775	4,812	4,074	4,337	4,766	3,601	3,805
Gen. and Admin.	2,876	1,874	1,882	2,820	1,783	1,872	3,222	1,672
Total Site Oper.								
Exp.	25,999	25,432	25,476	25,677	30,954	24,772	23,877	22,532
Physician Expenses:								
Physicians'								
Salaries	20,123	20,123	20,123	20,123	30,185	20,123	20,123	20,123
Payroll Taxes	992	992	992	992	992	992	992	992
Pension								
Expense	2,965	2.965	2,965	2,965	2,965	2,965	2,965	2,965
Physician								
Benefits	300	300	300	300	450	300	300	300
CME	333	333	333	333	333	333	333	333
Other Expenses	167	167	167	167	167	167	167	167
Total Phys.								
Expenses	24,880	24,880	24,880	24,880	35,092	24,880	24,880	24,880
Net Income before Physicians'								
Bonuses	14,594	21,716	22,222	10,893	(634)	22,230	5,556	9,986
Less: Debt								
Service	306	306	306	1,238	1,238	1,238	1,238	1,238
Less: Asset Acquisitions								
Site Cash Excess								
(Deficit)	14,288	21,410	21,916	9,655	(1,872)	20,992	4,318	8,748
Less: Central								
Admin Alloc	5,137	5,797	7,090	4,854	6,084	5,860	5,975	5,270
Net Cash Excess								
(Deficit)	9,151	15,613	14,825	4,801	(7,955)	15,132	(1,657)	3,478

	Sep	Oct	Nov	Dec	Totals	
Gross Charges	77,042	95,694	81,395	81,395	976,733	
Collection %	82.00%	82.00%	82.00%	82.00%	82.00%	
Collections	63,175	78,469	66,744	66,744	800,921	
Less: Refunds	(632)	(785)	(667)	(667)	(8,009)	
New Revenues	62,543	77,685	66,076	66,076	792,912	
Site Operating Expenses:						
Personnel Expenses	12,321	18,481	12,321	12,321	167,187	21.09%
Occupancy Costs	4,734	4,734	4,734	4,734	59,399	7.49%
Medical Expenses	4,147	5,150	4,381	4,381	52,570	6.63%
Gen. and Admin.	1,743	3,044	1,792	1,792	26,370	3.33%
Total Site Oper. Exp.	22,944	31,409	23,227	23,227	305,526	38.53%
Physician Expenses:						
Physicians' Salaries	20,123	30,185	20,123	20,123	261,602	32.99%
Payroll Taxes	992	992	992	992	11,903	1.50%
Pension Expense	2,965	2,965	2,965	2,965	35,578	4.49%
Physician Benefits	300	450	300	300	3,900	0.49%
CME	333	333	333	333	4,000	0.50%
Other Expenses	167	167	167	167	2,000	0.25%
Total Phys. Expenses	24,880	35,092	24,880	24,880	318,983	40.23%
Net Income before Physicians' Bonuses	14,719	11,184	17,969	17.969	168,403	21.24%
Less: Debt Service	1,238	1,238	1,238	1,238	12,058	1.52%
Less: Asset Acquisitions					0	0.00%
Site Cash Excess (Deficit)	13,481	9,946	16,731	16,731	156,345	19.72%
Less: Central Admin. Alloc.	6,018	8,981	6,036	6,143	73,246	9.24%
Net Cash Excess (Deficit)	7,463	965	10,695	10,588	83,099	10.48%

Sample Financial Statements

The Company
Balance Sheet
January 31, 2000

ASSETS

Current Assets		
Checking Account	$ 10,246.69	
Accounts Receivable	510,741.14	
Accounts Receivable-Reserve	<510,741.14>	
Total Current Assets		10,246.69
Property and Equipment		
Medical Equipment	21,438.96	
Accumulated Depr. - Med. Equip.	<1,191.79>	
Office Equipment	6,600.00	
Office Equipment - Accum. Depr.	<497.89>	
Computer Equipment	24,635.69	
Computer Equipment-Accum. Depr.	<1,448.73>	
Furniture & Fixtures	40,172.93	
Furniture & Fixtures-Accum.Depr.	<4,553.50>	
Total Property and Equipment		85,155.67
Other Assets		
Software	15,244.00	
Software-Accum Amort.	<2,117.23>	
Total Other Assets		13,126.77
Total Assets		$ 108,529.13

LIABILITIES AND CAPITAL

Current Liabilities		
Payroll - FICA	$ 616.78	
Payroll - FWH	1,379.24	

Cafeteria Withholding	<257.42>	
N/P - Bank	37,800.00	
Note Payable	17,757.00	
N/P - Furniture and Fixtures	4,214.58	
Total Current Liabilities		61,510.18
Long-Term Liabilities		
Total Long-Term Liabilities		0.00
Total Liabilities		61,510.18
Capital		
Retained Earnings	<23,995.05>	
Capital Contribution	71,014.00	
Net Income	0.00	
Total Capital		47,018.95
Total Liabilities & Capital		$ 108,529.13

Unaudited—For Management Purposes Only

The Company
Combined Income Statement
For the One Month and One Month Ending January 31, 2000

	Current Month Actual		Year to Date Actual	
Revenues				
AR Collections	$ 0.00	0.00	$ 0.00	0.00
AR Collections Unapplied	0.00	0.00	0.00	0.00
Chemo Collections	0.00	0.00	0.00	0.00
Lab Collections	0.00	0.00	0.00	0.00
Office Collections	0.00	0.00	0.00	0.00
Hospital Collections	0.00	0.00	0.00	0.00
Refunds - Patient	0.00	0.00	0.00	0.00
Refunds - Insurance Co.	0.00	0.00	0.00	0.00
Returned Checks	0.00	0.00	0.00	0.00
Net Revenue	0.00	0.00	0.00	0.00
Personnel Costs:				
Payroll: Comp FICA	0.00	0.00	0.00	0.00
Payroll: Comp FUTA	0.00	0.00	0.00	0.00
Payroll: Comp SUTA	0.00	0.00	0.00	0.00
Payroll: Gross	0.00	0.00	0.00	0.00
Temp Personnel	0.00	0.00	0.00	0.00
Health Insurance	0.00	0.00	0.00	0.00
Pension Expense	0.00	0.00	0.00	0.00
Total Personnel Costs	0.00	0.00	0.00	0.00
Fixed Expenses:				
Intermedia	0.00	0.00	0.00	0.00
Pagers	0.00	0.00	0.00	0.00
Computer Expense	0.00	0.00	0.00	0.00
Copier Expense	0.00	0.00	0.00	0.00
Corporate Entertainment	0.00	0.00	0.00	0.00
Amortization	0.00	0.00	0.00	0.00
Depreciation	0.00	0.00	0.00	0.00
Gifts & Donations	0.00	0.00	0.00	0.00
Late Fees	0.00	0.00	0.00	0.00
Marketing	0.00	0.00	0.00	0.00
Medical Supplies	0.00	0.00	0.00	0.00
Bank Charges	0.00	0.00	0.00	0.00
Credit Card Fees	0.00	0.00	0.00	0.00
Interest Expense	0.00	0.00	0.00	0.00
Discount Fees - Credit Card	0.00	0.00	0.00	0.00
Postage Equipment	0.00	0.00	0.00	0.00
Printer Expense	0.00	0.00	0.00	0.00

Professional Fees	0.00	0.00	0.00	0.00
Recruiting Expense	0.00	0.00	0.00	0.00
Rent	0.00	0.00	0.00	0.00
Travel - Staff	0.00	0.00	0.00	0.00
Total Fixed Expenses	0.00	0.00	0.00	0.00

Variable Expenses:

Answering Service	0.00	0.00	0.00	0.00
Telephone	0.00	0.00	0.00	0.00
Dues & Subs - Staff	0.00	0.00	0.00	0.00
Education - Staff	0.00	0.00	0.00	0.00
Fax Expense	0.00	0.00	0.00	0.00
Lab Service	0.00	0.00	0.00	0.00
Linens	0.00	0.00	0.00	0.00
Uniforms	0.00	0.00	0.00	0.00
Malpractice Insurance	0.00	0.00	0.00	0.00
Medications	0.00	0.00	0.00	0.00
Miscellaneous Expense	0.00	0.00	0.00	0.00
Misc. Tax Payment	0.00	0.00	0.00	0.00
Misc. Adjustments	0.00	0.00	0.00	0.00
Moving Expenses	0.00	0.00	0.00	0.00
Office Supplies	0.00	0.00	0.00	0.00

For Management Purposes Only

The Company Combined Income Statement
For the One Month and One Month Ending January 31, 2000

	Current Month Actual		Year to Date Actual	
Ins. - Prop, Casualty & WC	0.00	0.00	0.00	0.00
Payroll Expenses	0.00	0.00	0.00	0.00
Pension Expense	0.00	0.00	0.00	0.00
Petty Cash	0.00	0.00	0.00	0.00
Postage	0.00	0.00	0.00	0.00
Repairs & Maint.	0.00	0.00	0.00	0.00
TN Excise Taxes	0.00	0.00	0.00	0.00
Transcription	0.00	0.00	0.00	0.00
Total Variable Expenses	0.00	0.00	0.00	0.00
Total Operating Expenses	0.00	0.00	0.00	0.00
Income Before Physicians' Expenses	0.00	0.00	0.00	0.00
Physicians' Direct Expenses:				
Cellular	0.00	0.00	0.00	0.00
Disability Insurance	0.00	0.00	0.00	0.00
Physicians' Health Insurance	0.00	0.00	0.00	0.00
Physicians' Malpractice Ins.	0.00	0.00	0.00	0.00
Physicians' Dues & Subs	0.00	0.00	0.00	0.00
Physicians' Cont. Education	0.00	0.00	0.00	0.00
Physicians' Pension Expense	0.00	0.00	0.00	0.00
Physicians' Travel Expense	0.00	0.00	0.00	0.00
Total Physicians' Direct Expenses	0.00	0.00	0.00	0.00
Physicians' Compensation:				
Physicians' Salary	0.00	0.00	0.00	0.00
Physicians' Payroll Taxes	0.00	0.00	0.00	0.00
Total Physicians' Compensation	0.00	0.00	0.00	0.00
Other Income and (Expense):				
Interest Income	0.00	0.00	0.00	0.00
Miscellaneous Adjustment	0.00	0.00	0.00	0.00
Other Income	0.00	0.00	0.00	0.00
Management Fees	0.00	0.00	0.00	0.00
Other Income Allocation	0.00	0.00	0.00	0.00
Expense Reimbursement	0.00	0.00	0.00	0.00
Total Other Income and (Expense)	0.00	0.00	0.00	0.00
Net Income	$ 0.00	0.00	$ 0.00	0.00

For Management Purposes Only

APPENDIX D

Revenue Ruling 97-13

Rev. Proc. 97-13, 1997-5 I.R.B. 18.

INTERNAL REVENUE SERVICE
Revenue Procedure

TAX-EXEMPT BONDS; PRIVATE ACTIVITY BONDS

Released: January 10, 1997
Published: February 3, 1997

26 CFR 601.601: Rules and regulations.
Section 103. - Interest on State and Local Bonds
Section 141. - Private Activity Bond; Qualified Bond
26 CFR 1.141-3: Definition of private business use.
Section 145. - Qualified 501 (c) (3) Bonds
26 CFR 1.145-2: Application of private activity bond regulations.

Tax-exempt bonds; private activity bonds. This procedure sets forth conditions under which a management contract does not result in private business use under section 141 (b) of the Code. This procedure also applies to determinations of whether a management contract causes the test in section 145 (a) (2) (B) to be met for qualified 501 (c) (3) bonds.

SECTION 1. PURPOSE

The purpose of this revenue procedure is to set forth conditions under which a management contract does not result in private business use under § 141 (b) of the Internal Revenue Code of 1986. This revenue procedure also applies to determinations of whether a management contract causes the test in § 145 (a) (2) (B) of the 1986 Code to be met for qualified 501 (c) (3) bonds.

SECTION 2. BACKGROUND

.01 Private Business Use.

(1) Under § 103 (a) of the 1986 Code, gross income does not include interest on any state or local bond. Under § 103 (b) (1) of the 1986 Code, however, § 103 (a) of the 1986 Code does not apply to a private activity bond, unless it is a qualified bond under § 141 (e) of the 1986 Code. Section 141 (a) (1) of the 1986 Code defines "private activity bond" as any bond issued as part of an issue that meets both the private business use and the private security or payment tests. Under § 141 (b) (1) of the 1986 Code, an issue generally meets the private business use test if more than 10 percent of the proceeds of the issue are to be used for any private business use. Under § 141 (b) (6) (A) of the 1986 Code, private business use means direct or indirect use in a trade or business carried on by any person other than a government unit. Section 145 (a) of the 1986 Code also applies the private business use test of § 141 (b) (1) of the 1986 Code, with certain modifications.

(2) Corresponding provisions of the Internal Revenue Code of 1954 set forth the requirements for the exclusion from gross income of the interest on state or local bonds. For purposes of this revenue procedure, any reference to a 1986 Code provision includes a reference to the corresponding provision, if any, under the 1954 Code.

(3) Private business use can arise by ownership, actual or beneficial use of property pursuant to a lease, a management or incentive payment contract, or certain other arrangements. The Conference Report for the Tax Reform Act of 1986, provides as follows:

The conference agreement generally retains the present-law rules under which use by persons other than governmental units is determined for purposes of the trade or business use test. Thus, as under present law, the use of bond-financed property is treated as a use of bond proceeds. As under present law, a person may be a user of bond proceeds and bond-financed property as a result of (1) ownership or (2) actual or beneficial use of property pursuant to a lease, a management or incentive payment contract, or (3) any other arrangement such as a take-or-pay or other output-type contract. 2 H.R.Conf.Rep. No. 841, 99th Cong. 2d Sess. II-687-688, (1986) 1986-3 (Vol. 4) C.B. 6887-688 (footnote omitted).

(4) A management contract that gives a nongovernmental service provider an ownership or leasehold interest in financed property is not the only situation in which a contract may result in private business use.

(5) Section 1.141-3(b) (4) (i) of the Income Tax Regulations provides, in general, that a management contract (within the meaning of § 1.141-3 (b) (4) (ii)) with respect to financed property may result in private business use of that property, based on all the facts and circumstances.

(6) Section 1.141-3 (b) (4) (i) provides that a management contract with respect to financed property generally results in private business use of that property if the contract provides for compensation for services rendered with compensation based, in whole or in part, on a share of net profits from the operation of the facility.

(7) Section 1.141-3 (b) (4) (iii), in general, provides that certain arrangements generally are not treated as management contracts that may give rise to private business use. These are—

(a) Contracts for services that are solely incidental to the primary governmental function or functions of a financed facility (for example, contracts for janitorial, office equipment repair, hospital billing or similar services);

(b) The mere granting of admitting privileges by a hospital to a doctor, even if those privileges are conditioned on the provision of de minimis services, if those privileges are available to all qualified physicians in the area, consistent with the size and nature of its facilities;

(c) A contract to provide for the operation of a facility or system of facilities that consists predominantly of public utility property (as defined in § 168 (i) (10) of the 1986 Code), if the only compensation is the reimbursement of actual and direct expenses of the service provider and reasonable administrative overhead expenses of the service provider; and

(d) A contract to provide for services, if the only compensation is the reimbursement of the service provider for actual and direct expenses paid by the service provider to unrelated parties.

(8) Section 1.145-2 (a) provides generally that §§ 1.141-0 through 1.141-15 apply to § 145 (a) of the 1986 Code.

(9) Section 1.145-2 (b) (1) provides that in applying §§ 1.141-0 through 1.141-15 to § 145 (a) of the 1986 Code, references to governmental persons include section 501 (c) (3) organizations with respect to their activities that do not constitute unrelated trades or business under § 513 (a) of the 1986 Code.

.02 Existing Advance Ruling Guidelines. Rev. Proc. 93-19, 1993-1 C.B. 526, contains advance ruling guidelines for determining whether a management contract results in private business use under § 141 (b) of the 1986 Code.

SECTION 3. DEFINITIONS

.01 Adjusted gross revenues means gross revenues of all or a portion of a facility, less allowances for bad debts and contractual and similar allowances.

.02 Capitation fee means a fixed periodic amount for each person for whom the service provider or the qualified user assumes the responsibility to provide all needed services for a specified period so long as the quantity and type of services actually provided to covered persons varies substantially. For example, a capitation fee includes a fixed dollar amount payable per month to a medical service provider for each member of a health maintenance organization plan for whom the provider agrees to provide all needed medical services for a specified period. A capitation fee may include a variable component of up to 20 percent of the total capitation fee designed to protect the service provider against risks such as catastrophic loss.

.03 Management contract means a management, service, or incentive payment contract between a qualified user and a service provider under which the service provider provides services involving all, a portion of, or any function of, a facility. For example, a contract for the provision of management services for an entire hospital, a contract for management services for a specific department of a hospital, and an incentive payment contract for physician services to patients of a hospital are each treated as a management contract. See §§ 1.141-3 (b) (4) (ii) and 1.145-2.

.04 Penalties for terminating a contract include a limitation on the qualified user's right to compete with the service provider; a requirement that the qualified user purchase equipment, goods, or services from the service provider; and a requirement that the qualified user pay liquidated damages for cancellation of the contract. In contrast, a requirement effective on cancellation that the qualified user reimburse the service provider for ordinary and necessary expenses or a restriction on the qualified user against hiring key personnel of the service provider is generally not a contract termination penalty. Another contract between the service provider and the qualified user, such as a loan or guarantee by the service provider, is treated as creating a contract termination penalty if that contract contains terms that are not customary or arm's- length that could operate to prevent the qualified user from terminating the contract (for example, provisions under which the contract terminates if the management contract is terminated or that place substantial restrictions on the selection of a substitute service provider).

.05 Periodic fixed fee means a stated dollar amount for services rendered for a specified period of time. For example, a stated dollar amount per month is a periodic fixed fee. The stated dollar amount may automatically increase according to a specified, objective, external standard that is not linked to the output or efficiency of a facility. For example, the Consumer Price Index and similar external indices that track increases in prices in an area or increases in revenues or costs in an industry are objective external standards. Capitation fees and per-unit fees are not periodic fixed fees.

.06 Per-unit fee means a fee based on a unit of service provided specified in the contract or otherwise specifically determined by an independent third party, such as the administrator of the Medicare program, or the qualified user. For example, a stated dollar amount for each specified medical procedure performed, car parked, or passenger mile is a per-unit fee. Separate billing arrangements between physicians and hospitals generally are treated as per-unit fee arrangements.

.07 Qualified user means any state or local governmental unit as defined in § 1.103-1 or any instrumentality thereof. The term also includes a section 501 (c) (3) organization if the financed property is not used in an unrelated trade or business under § 513 (a) of the 1986 Code. The term does not include the United States or any agency or instrumentality thereof.

.08 Renewal option means a provision under which the service provider has a legally enforceable right to renew the contract. Thus, for example, a provision under which a contract is automatically renewed for one-year periods absent cancellation by either party is not a renewal option (even if it is expected to be renewed).

.09 Service provider means any person other than a qualified user that provides services under a contract to, or for the benefit of, a qualified user.

SECTION 4. SCOPE

This revenue procedure applies when, under a management contract, a service provider provides management or other services involving property financed with proceeds of an issue of state or local bonds subject to § 141 or § 145 (a) (2) (B) of the 1986 Code.

SECTION 5. OPERATING GUIDELINES FOR MANAGEMENT CONTRACTS

.01 In general. If the requirements of section 5 of this revenue procedure are satisfied, the management contract does not itself result in private business use. In addition, the use of financed property, pursuant to a management contract meeting the requirements of section 5 of this revenue procedure, is not private business use if that use is functionally related and subordinate to that management contract and that use is not, in substance, a separate contractual agreement (for example, a separate lease of a portion of the financed property). Thus, for example, exclusive use of storage areas by the manager for equipment that is necessary for it to perform activities required under a management contract that meets the requirements of section 5 of this revenue procedure, is not private business use.

.02 General compensation requirements.

(1) In general. The contract must provide for reasonable compensation for services rendered with no compensation based, in whole or in part, on a share of net profits from the operation of the facility. Reimbursement of the service provider for actual and direct expenses paid by the service provider to unrelated parties is not by itself treated as compensation.

(2) Arrangements that generally are not treated as net profits arrangements. For purposes of § 1.141-3 (b) (4) (i) and this revenue procedure, compensation based on:

(a) A percentage of gross revenues (or adjusted gross revenues) of a facility or a percentage of expenses from a facility, but not both;

(b) A capitation fee; or

(c) A per-unit fee is generally not considered to be based on a share of net profits.

(3) Productivity reward. For purposes of § 1.141-3 (b) (4) (i) and this revenue procedure, a productivity reward equal to a stated dollar amount based on increases or decreases in gross revenues (or adjusted gross revenues), or reductions in total expenses (but not both increases in gross revenues (or adjusted gross revenues) and reductions in total expenses) in any annual period during the term of the contract, generally does not cause the compensation to be based on a share of net profits.

(4) Revision of compensation arrangements. In general, if the compensation arrangements of a management contract are materially revised, the requirements for compensation arrangements under section 5 of this revenue procedure are retested as of the date of the material revision, and the management contract is treated as one that was newly entered into as of the date of the material revision.

.03 Permissible Arrangements. The management contract must be described in section 5.03 (1), (2), (3), (4), (5), or (6) of this revenue procedure.

(1) 95 percent periodic fixed fee arrangements. At least 95 percent of the compensation for services for each annual period during the tern of the contract is based on a periodic fixed fee. The term of the contract, including all renewal options, must not exceed the lesser of 80 percent of the reasonably expected useful life of the financed property and 15 years. For purposes of this section 5.03 (1), a fee does not fail to qualify as a periodic fixed fee as a result of a one-time incentive award during the term of the contract under which compensation automatically increases when a gross revenue or expense target (but not both) is reached if that award is equal to a single, stated dollar amount.

(2) 80 percent periodic fixed fee arrangements. At least 80 percent of the compensation for services for each annual period during the term of the contract is based on a periodic fixed fee. The term of the contract, including all renewal options, must not exceed the lesser of 80 percent of the reasonably expected useful life of the financed property and 10 years. For purposes of this section 5.03 (2), a fee does not fail to qualify as a periodic fixed fee as a result of a one-time incentive award during the term of the contract under which compensation automatically increases when a gross revenue or expense target (but not both) is reached if that award is equal to a single, stated dollar amount.

(3) Special rule for public utility property. If all of the financed property subject to the contract is a facility or system of facilities consisting of predominantly public utility property (as defined in § 168 (i) (10) of the 1986 Code), then "20 years" is substituted:

(a) For "15 years" in applying section 5.03 (1) of this revenue procedure; and

(b) For "10 years" in applying section 5.03 (2) of this revenue procedure.

(4) 50 percent periodic fixed fee arrangements. Either at least 50 percent of the compensation for services for each annual period during the term of the contract is based on a periodic fixed fee or all of the compensation for services is based on a capitation fee or a combination of a capitation fee and a periodic fixed fee. The term of the contract, including all renewal options, must not exceed 5 years. The contract must be terminable by the qualified user on reasonable notice, without penalty or cause, at the end of the third year of the contract term.

(5) Per-unit fee arrangements in certain 3-year contracts. All of the compensation for services is based on a per-unit fee or a combination of a per-unit fee and a periodic fixed fee. The term of the contract, including all renewal options, must not exceed 3 years. The contract must be terminable by the

qualified user on reasonable notice, without penalty or cause, at the end of the second year of the contract term.

(6) Percentage of revenue or expense fee arrangements in certain 2-year contracts. All the compensation for services is based on a percentage of fees charged or a combination of a per-unit fee and a percentage of revenue or expense fee. During the start-up period, however, compensation may be based on a percentage of either gross revenues, adjusted gross revenues, or expenses of a facility. The term of the contract, including renewal options, must not exceed 2 years. The contract must be terminable by the qualified user on reasonable notice, without penalty or cause, at the end of the first year of the contract term. This section 5.03 (6) applies only to:

(a) Contracts under which the service provider primarily provides services to third parties (for example, radiology services to patients); and

(b) Management contracts involving a facility during an initial start-up period for which there have been insufficient operations to establish a reasonable estimate of the amount of the annual gross revenues and expenses (for example, a contract for general management services for the first year of operations).

.04 No Circumstances Substantially Limiting Exercise of Rights

(1) In general. The service provider must not have any role or relationship with the qualified user that, in effect, substantially limits the qualified user's ability to exercise its rights, including cancellation rights, under the contract, based on all the facts and circumstances.

(2) Safe harbor. This requirement is satisfied if:

(a) Not more than 20 percent of the voting power of the governing body of the qualified user in the aggregate is vested in the service provider and its directors, officers, shareholders, and employees;

(b) Overlapping board members do not include the chief executive officers of the service provider or its governing body or the qualified user or its governing body; and

(c) The qualified user and the service provider under the contract are not related parties, as defined in § 1.150-1 (b).

SECTION 6. EFFECT ON OTHER DOCUMENTS

Rev. Proc. 93-19, 1993-1 C.B. 526, is made obsolete on the effective date of this revenue procedure.

SECTION 7. EFFECTIVE DATE

This revenue procedure is effective for any management contract entered into, materially modified, or extended (other than pursuant to a renewal option) on or after May 16, 1997. In addition, an issuer may apply this revenue procedure to any management contract entered into prior to May 16, 1997.

DRAFTING INFORMATION

The principal author of this revenue procedure is Loretta J. Finger of the Office of Assistant Chief Counsel (Financial Institutions and Products). For further information regarding this revenue procedure contact Loretta J. Finger on (202) 622-3980 (not a toll-free call).

Rev. Proc. 97-13, 1997-5 I.R.B. 18.

APPENDIX E

Glossary of Terms

Assignment of Benefits—The payment of medical benefits directly to a provider of care rather than to a member or beneficiary.

Balance Billing—The practice of a provider billing a patient for all charges not paid for by the insurance plan, even if those charges are above the plan's UCR or are considered medically unnecessary.

Capitation—A method of paying for medical services on a per-person rather than a per-procedure basis. Under capitation, an HMO pays a participating doctor a fixed amount per month for every HMO member he or she takes care of, regardless of how much or how little care the member receives.

Closed Panel—A managed care plan that contracts with physicians on an exclusive basis for services and does not allow those physicians to see patients from another managed care organization.

Continuous Quality Improvement (CQI)—These are programs intended to reduce the number of variations in healthcare treatment and outcomes. The principles of CQI involve defining quality throughout the organization in both clinical operations and service processes. The approach involves the development of critical pathways depicting the process of a patient with a particular diagnosis moving through a healthcare organization; these pathways are intended to reduce resource use and lengths of stay.

Copayment—A fixed payment the patient pays (usually in the $5 to $25 range) each time he or she visits a health plan clinician or receives a covered service.

Deductible—More typical in traditional health insurance, a fixed amount the patient must pay each year before the insurer will begin covering the cost of care.

Fee for service—The traditional method of paying for medical services. A doctor charges a fee for each service provided, and the insurer pays all or part of that fee. Sometimes the patient pays a copayment for each visit to the doctor.

FTE (Full-time Equivalent)—The equivalent of one full-time employee.

HCFA (Health Care Financing Administration)—The federal agency that oversees all aspects of health financing for Medicare.

Health Maintenance Organization (HMO)—An organization that provides healthcare in return for preset monthly payments. Most HMOs provide care through a network of doctors, hospitals, and other medical professionals that their members must use in order to be covered for that care. There are several types of HMO models, including:

> **Staff Model HMO**—A type of HMO in which the doctors and other medical professionals are salaried employees of the HMO, and the clinics or health center in which they practice are owned by the HMO.

> **Group Model HMO**—A model of HMO made up of one or more physician group practices that are not owned by the HMO but that operate as independent partnerships or professional corporations. The HMO pays the groups at a negotiated rate, and each group is responsible for paying its doctors and other staff and for paying for hospital care or care from outside specialists.

> **Independent Practice Association (IPA)**—IPAs generally include large numbers of individual private practice physicians who are paid either a fee or a fixed amount per patient to take care of the IPA's members.

> **Mixed Model HMO:** A health plan that includes more than one form of HMO within a single plan. For instance, a group model HMO might also contract with independent physician groups or with individual private practice physicians.

Health Employer Data and Information Set (HEDIS)—HEDIS provides a set of performance measures for employers and other purchasers of health plans to understand and evaluate a health plan's performance.

Managed Care Organization—An umbrella term for HMOs and all health plans that provide healthcare in return for preset monthly payments and coordinate care through a defined network of primary care physicians and hospitals.

Management Service Organization (MSO)—An entity that provides a variety of assets and services to one or more medical practices.

Medicare—An entitlement program run by the Health Care Financing Administration (HCFA) of the federal government by which people 65 years or older receive health care insurance. Medicare Part A covers hospitalization and is a compulsory benefit. Medicare Part B covers outpatient services and is a voluntary service.

Medicaid—An entitlement program run by both the state and federal government for the provision of health care insurance to patients younger than 65 years who cannot afford to pay private health insurance.

Medical Group Practice—The provision of healthcare services by three or more physicians who are formally organized as a legal entity governed by physicians in which business, clinical and administrative facilities, records, and personnel are shared and the practice goals, objectives, and values are commonly defined. Income from medical services provided by the group are treated as receipts of the group and distributed according to some prearranged plan.

Network—The doctors, clinics, health centers, medical group practices, hospitals, and other providers that an HMO, PPO, or other managed care network plan has selected and contracted with to care for its members.

Outcomes Management—A systematic approach to improve the quality of healthcare and reduce variations through the documentation of treatment effectiveness. Outcomes management identifies outliers and informs physicians so that they can change their behavior.

Out of Network—Not in the HMO's network of selected and approved doctors and hospitals. HMO members who get care out of network (sometimes called out of area) without getting permission from the HMO to do so may have to pay for all or most of that care themselves. Exceptions are usually made for extreme emergencies or urgent care needed when traveling away from home.

Physician-Hospital Organization (PHO)—A legal (or perhaps informal) organization that links hospitals and the attending medical staff. PHOs frequently are developed for the purpose of contracting with managed care plans.

Physician Organization—A general term used to refer to a variety of newly forming physicians' entities developing, such as specialty networks, integrated group practices, and the physician equity model.

Point-of-Service (POS) plan—A type of HMO coverage that allows members to choose to receive services either from participating HMO providers or from providers outside the HMO's network. In-network care is more fully covered; for out-of-network care, members pay deductibles and a percentage of the cost of care, much like traditional health insurance coverage.

Preferred Provider Organization (PPO)—A network of doctors and hospitals that provides care at a lower cost than through traditional insurance.

PPO members get better benefits (more coverage) when they use the PPO's network and pay higher out-of-pocket costs when they receive care outside the PPO network.

Preventive Care—Care designed to prevent disease altogether, to detect and treat it early, or to manage its course most effectively. Examples of preventive care include immunizations and regular screenings like Pap smears or cholesterol checks.

Primary Care—Preventive healthcare and routine medical care that typically is provided by a doctor trained in internal medicine, pediatrics, or family practice, or by a nurse, nurse practitioner, or physician's assistant.

Primary Care Physician (PCP)—A physician, usually an internist, pediatrician, or family physician, devoted to general medical care of patients. Most HMOs require members to choose a primary care physician, who is then expected to provide or authorize all care for that patient.

Referral—A formal process that authorizes an HMO member to get care from a specialist or hospital. To assure coverage, an HMO patient generally must get a referral from his or her primary care doctor before seeing a specialist.

Resourced Based Relative Value System (RBRVS)—A relative value scale developed for HCFA for use by Medicare. The RBRVS assigns relative values to each CPT code for services on the basis of the resources related to the procedure rather than simply on analysis of historical trends.

Specialist—A doctor or other health professional whose training and expertise are in a specific area of medicine, such as cardiology or dermatology. Most HMOs require members to get a referral from their primary care physician before seeing a specialist.

Usual, Customary, or Reasonable (UCR)—A method of profiling prevailing fees in an area and reimbursing providers on the basis of that profile.

Withhold Fund—The portion of the monthly capitation payment to physicians withheld by the HMO or other managed care plan until the end of the year (or other period) to create an incentive for efficient care.

References

1999 Cost Survey. Englewood, CO: MGMA, 1999.

1999 Management Compensation Survey. Englewood, CO: MGMA, 1999.

1999 Physician Compensation & Production Survey. Englewood, CO: MGMA 1999.

Aust, Marilee. "Emphasize Performance, Not Just Productivity, in Compensation." *Medical Group Management Update,* 36(5), May 1997, 11.

Barry, Dennis M. "Stark—Considerations in Financial Relationships," Presentation outline, 1998.

Becker, Scott. "Current Approaches to Physician Compensation." *Bender's Health Care Law Monthly,* 12(9), September 1997, 3–9

Bok, Derek. *The Cost of Talent.* New York: The Free Press 1993.

Cejka, Susan, and Lesley Coleman. "Don't Get Decapitated by a Poor Physician Compensation Plan." *Today's Internist,* 38(2), March/April 1997, 12–18.

"Coming of Age." *Modern Physician,* No. 11, December 1997, 33–34.

"Compensation Plan Hinges on Appropriateness of Care." *Capitation Management Report,* 3(2) February 1996, 17–21.

Cunningham, Carl. "Goldilocks and the Bears' Compensation System: Is There One 'Just Right'?" *Today's Internist,* 38(5), September/October 1997, 42–43.

"Customize Physician Incentive Programs to Fit the Individual Doctors' Needs." *Medical Network Strategy Report,* 5(6), May 1996, 4–7

Ekrem, Martin R. "Making the Tough Call: Cost Cutting, Physician Compensation, and Other Difficult Decisions." *Group Practice Journal,* July/August 1998.

Farrell, James. "Physician Executive Contracts: Negotiating the Future." *Physician Executive,* 21(9), September 1995, 25–29.

Flannery, Thomas P., David A. Hofrichter, and Paul E. Platten. *People, Performance & Pay.* New York: The Free Press, 1996.

Koeppen, Linda, Michael Mess, Kara Trott, and Linda Yazvac. "Aligning Incentives for Success." *Physician Executive*, 23(1), January 1997, 14–19.

Korenchuk, Keith M. *Transforming the Delivery of Health Care: The Integration Process.* Englewood, CO: MGMA, 1994.

Krill, Mary Alice. *Successful Partnerships for the Future: Administrator-Physician Dynamics.* Englewood, CO: MGMA, 1995.

Krohn, Arthur. "Provider Compensation in the Academic Group Practice," Paper, American College of Medical Practice Executives, 1996.

Lawler, Edward E. III. *Strategic Pay; Aligning Organizational Strategies and Pay Systems.* San Francisco, CA: Jossey-Bass, 1990.

Lloyd, John S., and Mary Frances Lyons. "The Physician Executive 'Arrives'—A New Generation Prepares for the Future." *Physician Executive*, 21(1), January 1995, 22–26.

Lowenhaupt, Manuel T. "Building Strategic, Value-Based Compensation Models that Really Get the Results You Want: Make the Reward Worth the Effort." *Physician's Management*, 37(9), September 1997, 50–54.

Lyons, Mary Frances, Dan Ford, and Glenn Singer. "How Do Physician Executives View Themselves?" *Physician Executive*, 22(9), September 1996, 23–26.

"MD Payment Plans Continue to Evolve Under Capitation." *Capitation Management Report*, 4(6), June 1997, 89–96.

Mess, Michael. "Structuring Physician Compensation Arrangements: Traveling Through the Maze of Regulatory Requirements," Presentation Outline.

Moore, Pamela L. "Compensation Options Numerous under Managed Care." *Medical Group Management*, 36(7), July 15, 1997, 2.

Oppenheim, Charles B. *Stark II Regulations: A Comprehensive Analysis.* Washington, DC: American Health Lawyers Association, 1998.

Owens, James F., and Michael A. Wilson. *Physician Compensation Issues.* Washington, DC: American Health Lawyers Association, 1999.

Peters, Gerald R. *Healthcare Integration: A Legal Manual for Constructing Integrated Organizations.* Washington, DC: NHLA, 1995.

Raczak, Theresa. "Physician Compensation: Designing a Plan Within a Capitated Environment." *Journal of Medical Practice Management*, 11(6), May 1996, 265–268.

RBRVS Fee Schedule: A Plain-English Guide. Rockville, MD: Part B News Group, 1999.

Reidboldt, J. Max. *Physician Compensation Systems.* Norcross, GA: Coker Publishing, LLC, 1999.

Relative Values for Physicians. New York: McGraw-Hill, 1995.

Swander, Holly. "RVU-to-Visit Ratios Can Reveal Productivity Trends." *Medical Group Management*, 37(1), June 1, 1998, 1.

Wallen, Eileen. "Physician-CEO's Blend Skills." *Physician's Financial News*, 16(2), February 15, 1998, §31–32.

Yenney, Sharon L. *Evaluating and Negotiating Your Compensation Arrangements.* AMA, 1998.

Index

Academic practices, 139–144
  complications in, 139–140
  parameters of, 140
  regulatory considerations of,
    140–144
Accounts payable, net cash available
  and, 28–29
Accrual basis accounting, 29
Adjusted charges, 110–111
Administration, *see* Compensation, plan
  administration; Management
  activities; Medical director
Alabama, 13
Ambulatory surgery centers, safe
  harbor for, 40
Antikickback statute, 37–38
  academic practices and, 143
  MSOs and, 147–148
  safe harbors in, 38–44

Balance billing, 22
Base salary, 83–93
  for academic practices, 140
  budget and, 85–90
  factors in determining, 90–93
Benefit plans, 101–108
  in employment agreement,
    77–78
  for retirement, 103–108
  typical, 101–103
Bonus:
  as compensation, 84
  defined, 31

Budget:
  capital, 89–90
  expenses and, 88
  preparation of, 85
  revenues and, 86–88
  sample, 180–182
Business knowledge, need for, 158–159

C corporations, 64
Cafeteria benefit plans, 102
California, 114
Call rotation, base salary and, 90–91
Capital budget, 89–90
Capitation payments:
  budgets and, 88
  impact of, 6, 7, 8–10
  incentives and, 9–10
  RVUs and, 123–124
Case studies, 164–165
  of internal medicine practice,
    165–170
  of surgical group, 170–175
Cash balance plan, 106–107
Cash basis accounting, 29
CEO, *see* Medical director
Charges:
  adjusted, 110–111
  gross, 109–110
  Medicare limits on, 23
Civil monetary penalties (CMP) law,
  gainsharing and, 97–98
Collections, 86–88
  academic practices and, 144

Collections, 86–88 (*Continued*)
  adjusted gross charges and, 111
  as productivity measure, 111
Commercial payors, 25
Committee responsibilities, of medical
    director, 161
Compensation:
  basic components of, 62
  basic principles, 56–61
  defined, 45
  financial implications of, 7–10
  plan administration, 133–138
Competition, impact of, 26–27
Confidential information, nondisclosure
    of, 80
Consumers, *see* Patients
Continuing medical education benefits,
    102
Contract, *see* Employment agreements
Control-of-utilization methods, impact
    of, 6
Conversion factors, RVUs and, 120
Costs, *see* Expenses
Current Procedural Terminology (CPT)
    codes, 112, 115, 121–122
Customary, prevailing, and reasonable
    charges, 22, 25

De minimis compensation, regulatory
    considerations, 53–54
Debt:
  in budgeting, 89–90
  cash flow and, 29
Defined benefit retirement plan, 103, 106
Defined contribution retirement plan,
    103, 105–106
DeParle, Nancy-Ann, 14
Department of Health Human and
    Services (DHHS), 13, 141
Department of Justice, 141
Depreciation, 29–30
Designated health services, *see* Health
    services
Direct expenses, 126–127, 132
Disability insurance, 102, 108
Discounted fee-for-service payments, 6,
    7, 8

Discounts, regulatory considerations,
    54–55
Dividend payments, salaries reclassified
    as, 72–73
Dues/fees, as benefit, 102

"Eat what you kill," 30, 109
Efficiency, incentives and, 97
Employees, safe harbor for, 38
Employment agreements, 75–82
  protections of, 75–76
  standard content of, 77–82
Equal compensation, 164–165
Equipment, *see* Space/equipment rental
Ethics in Patient Referrals Act of 1989,
    see Stark I and II
Evaluation, of physicians, 137, 160–161
Evergreen contract, 77
Expense allowances, as benefit,
    102–103
Expenses:
  allocation of, 15, 125–130, 178
  budget and, 88
  equal, 127–128
  impact of, 18
  incentives to control, 95, 98
  increases in, 26
  per RVU, 124
  trends in, 26

False Claims Act (FCA), 154
Federal restrictions, *see* Regulatory
    considerations
Fee-for-service payments, impact of
    discounted, 6, 7, 8
Fees/dues, as benefit, 102
Financial relationship, defined, 45
Financial statements, 31
  capitation's impact on, 9
  sample, 183–187
Fixed expenses, 88
Followers, physicians as, 156–157
Foundation model, of physician
    integration system, 148–150
Fraud/abuse, regulatory
    considerations, 37–44
Fringe benefits, *see* Benefit plans

Gainsharing:
    incentives and, 97–98
    IRS and, 36
Gatekeeper, 16, 130
General partnerships, tax considerations
    for, 62–63
Geographic practice cost index (GPCI),
    23–24, 119–120
Government regulation, *see* Regulatory
    considerations
Gross charges, productivity and,
    109–110
Gross national product (GNP), 25
Group practice:
    mergers of, 15–16
    MSOs and, 149–150
    new physicians in, 83–84
    referrals within, 46
    Stark I and II and, 49–53

Health Care Financing Administration
    (HCFA), 24
Health insurance, 101
Health maintenance organization
    (HMO), 25
Health professional shortage areas
    (HSPAs), 39
Health Security Act of 1993, 1–2
    problems described in, 11–12
Health services, Stark and, 46–47, 149
HEDIS (Health Plan Employer Data and
    Information Set), 12–13, 97
Highly compensated employees
    (HCEs), retirement and, 103–104
*Homebound Medical Care v. Hospital
    Staffing Services*, 81–82
Hospital incentive arrangements, 98
Hospital-owned physician practice
    model, *see* Integrated delivery
    system
Hsiao, William C., 115

Immediate family, defined, 45
In-office ancillary exception, to Stark, 49
Incentive compensation, 94–100
    for academic practices, 140, 144
    base salary and, 84

in capitated environment, 9–10
defined, 31
in employment agreement, 75
IRS and, 98–99
mergers and, 16
pitfalls of, 177–178
productivity and, 95–96
purpose/objectives of, 94–95
typical, 33–34
Indemnity plans:
    decrease in reimbursement from, 25
    described, 7
Indirect costs, 132, 144
Insiders, physicians as, 33
Insurance companies, profiling by,
    13–14
Insurance:
    as benefit, 101, 102, 108
    conversion of, at termination, 108
    malpractice, 40
    patients' lack of, 11
Integrated delivery system, 150–154
    models of, 151–152
    regulatory considerations of, 152–154
Internal medicine practice case study,
    165–170
Internal Revenue Service (IRS):
    academic practices and, 143
    501(c)(3) organizations, 33
    incentive compensation and, 98–99
    integrated delivery system and,
        152–154
    Rev. Proc. 93-19, 36
    Rev. Proc. 97-13, 36
    Rev. Ruling 97-13, 188–196
Investment interests, 39, 48
Iowa, 13

Joint ventures, safe harbor for, 39

Kickbacks, *see* Antikickback statute

Leader, of practice, 133–134. *See also*
    Medical director
    abilities of effective, 155–156
    characteristics of, 134–136
    role of, 136–137

Legal liability, general partnerships and, 63
Life insurance, 101, 108
Limited liability companies (LLCs), tax considerations of, 63
Lump-sum assets, retirement and, 104–105

Malpractice RVUs, 119
Managed care:
  budgets and, 88
  impact of, 6
Management activities, 136–137, 160. *See also* Medical director
  base salary and, 92
  in employment agreement, 78–79
Management contracts:
  MSOs and, 148
  Rev. Proc. 97-13 and, 36
  safe harbors for, 38
Management services organization (MSO) model, of physician integration system, 146–148
Maximum allowable actual charges (MAAC), 23
McGraw-Hill Relative Values for Physicians, 25, 114
Medicaid:
  collections and, 111
  decreases in reimbursements from, 24
  designated health service for, 46
  gainsharing and, 36
  gross charges and, 110
Medical director, *see also* Management activities
  continuing education needs of, 158–159
  importance of leadership by, 155–158
  practice administrator and, 157–158
  responsibilities of, 159–161
Medical Group Management Association survey:
  on capitation, 9–10
  on collections, 25
  on costs, 26
  on general partnerships, 63
  IRS use of, 71

on LLCs, 63
on medical director compensation, 162
on professional corporations, 64
as sanity check, 86–87
on specialists, 16
Medical schools, *see* Academic practices
Medical students, 141
Medically underserved areas (MUAs), 39
Medicare:
  academic practices and, 141–143
  decreases in reimbursements from, 21–24
  gainsharing and, 36
  integrated delivery system and, 151–152
  medical foundation and, 150
  MSOs and, 147
  participation/nonparticipation in, 22–24
  Stark I and II and, 44–45
Merger/integration of practice:
  employment agreements and, 76
  impact of, 14–17
Money purchase plan, 105
Multispecialty practice mergers, 16–17

National Committee for Quality Assurance (NCQA), 12–13
  web site of, 13
National Institutes of Health, 141
National Provider Identification Number (NPIN), 13
Net cash available, 28–29
Net income, 29–30
  compensation in excess of, 176–177
New York, 13
Noncompete agreements, 79–82
Nonqualified retirement plans, 108
Notice of Proposed Rulemaking (NPRM), 13

Obstetrical malpractice insurance, safe harbor for, 40
Ohio, 13
Omnibus Budget Reconciliation Act (OBRA) of 1989, 23

Outcomes measurement, 12–14
Outliers, 14
Overhead, *see* Costs

Pacificare Health System, 13
Parent holding company model, of
    integrated delivery system, 151
Partnership, National Health Lawyers
    Association's definition of, 3
Patients:
    demands of, 10–14
    retention of, 81
    satisfaction of, 95, 97
    volume of, 91–92, 96
Pension plan, *see* Nonqualified
    retirement plans; Qualified
    retirement plans
Per member per month (PMPM), 8–9
Personal service corporations, 64
Personnel costs, 26
Physician controlled model, of
    integrated delivery system, 151
Physician-hospital organizations
    (PHOs), 145
Physicians:
    evaluation/management of, 137,
        160–161
    hiring of new, 92
    incentives for recruitment of, 95
Physicians integration systems,
    145–154
    foundation model, 148–150
    hospital-owned physician practice
        model, 150–154
    management services organization
        (MSO) model, 146–148
Point-of-service plans (POS), impact of, 7
Points system, for productivity
    measurement, 112–113
Practice, *see also* Management activities;
    Medical director
    objective analysis of, 20–21
    organizational structure of, 136–138
    policies/procedures of, 137
Practice administrator, 157–158
Practice expense portion, of RVU, 24, 118
Price fixing, 114

Primary care:
    capitation and income, 10
    oversupply of physicians, 26–27
Prior year allocation method, 129–131
Private inurement, 33–35, 143–144
Product development, impact of, 7
Productivity:
    incentives and, 95–96
    measuring of, 109–113
Professional corporations, tax
    considerations for, 64–74
Profiling, 13–14
Profit-sharing plan, 105
Public benefit requirement, 33

Qualifications, base salary and, 90
Qualified retirement plans, 101
    cash balance, 106–107
    defined benefit, 103, 106
    defined contribution, 103, 105–106
    lump sum needs estimate for, 104–105
    tax consequences of, 103–104
Quality, 12
    incentives and, 97
    medical director and, 161
    private measures of, 13
    public measures of, 12–13, 14

Recruitment agreements:
    regulatory considerations, 33–35
    safe harbor for, 39–40
Referrals, *see* Antikickback statute
Regulatory considerations, 32
    de minimis compensation, 53–54
    discounts, 54–55
    fraud/abuse, 37–44
    impact of, 17–18
    recruitment agreements, 33–35
    Stark I and II, 44–53
    tax-exempt financing, 35–36
    tax-exempt organizations, 33
Reimbursement, decreases in, 21
Relative Value for Physicians (RVPs), 114
Relative value units (RVUs), 112,
    114–116
    calculation of, 115
    conversion factors, 120

Relative value units (RVUs) (*Continued*)
   establishment of, 114–115
   geographic practice cost index and,
     119–120
   malpractice portion, 119
   practice expense portion, 24, 118
   productivity measurement and,
     121–124
   work portion, 116–118
Remuneration, defined, 45
Rentals, *see* Space/equipment rental
Repayment, of subsidy, 34–35
Residents, Medicare billing and,
   141–142
Resource-based relative value scale
   (RBVS), 22
   fee schedule of, 23–24
   productivity and, 96
   relative value unit portion of, 24
Resources:
   incentives to manage, 96–97
   investing in practice, 89–90
Restrictive covenant, in employment
   agreement, 79–82
Retirement plans, *see* Nonqualified
   retirement plans; Qualified
   retirement plans
Revenue "pie":
   decline in, 20–27
   defined, 28–31
Revenues, *see* Collections; Revenue
   "pie"
Richlands Medical Association v.
   Commissioner, 64–70
Risk/reward, 6, 7, 8
RVUs, *see* Relative value units
   (RVUs)

S corporations, 73
Safe harbors, in antikickback statute,
   38–44
Sale of practice, safe harbor for,
   38, 40
Self-referral laws, *see* Stark I and II
Single organization model, of integrated
   delivery system, 151
Sinsheimer, JoAnne, 45

Solo physicians, mergers of, 15
Space/equipment rental:
   MSOs and, 147–148
   safe harbor for, 38–39
   suspect arrangements, 41–44
Specialty practices:
   capitation and, 10
   income declines in, 26
   safe harbor for, 41
Split-dollar life insurance, 108
Stark I and II, 44–53
   cost allocation and, 131–132
   exceptions to, 47–53
   impact of, 17–18
   integrated delivery system and,
     151–152
   in internal medicine case study,
     166–170
   medical foundation and,
     149–150
Stark, Peter, 2
State restrictions, *see* Regulatory
   considerations
Stockholder loan, 74
Sub S corporations, 64
"Substantially all," defined, 150
Surgical group case study,
   170–175

Tax considerations:
   of benefit plans, 101–103
   for exempt organizations, 33
   of financing, 35–36
   for general partnerships, 62–63
   for limited liability companies,
     63
   for professional corporations,
     64–74
   of retirement plans, 103–108
Teaching hospitals, *see* Academic
   practices
Tennessee, 13
Tenure, base salary and, 90
Termination provisions:
   in employment agreement, 82,
     108
   insurance conversion and, 108

Top-heavy retirement plan, 104, 106
Towers Perrin Healthcare Cost Survey
(2000), 18

Unique provider identification number
(UPIN), 13
*United States v. American Associates of
Anesthesiologists*, 114
Utilization:
capitation and, 10
cost allocation and, 127–128
as performance measure, 137

Vacation benefits, 102
Variable expenses, 88, 128–129
Vesting, 104
Vladeck, Bruce C., 12

Weighted average production,
112
Withholds, 6, 8
Work hours, base salary and,
90–91
Work RVUs, 116–118
updating of, 117–118